DEBOR

Meant for Good

Fundamentals of Womanist Leadership

Foreword by Cheryl Townsend Gilkes

JUDSON PRESS
PUBLISHERS SINCE 1824
VALLEY FORGE, PA

Meant for Good: Fundamentals of Womanist Leadership
© 2019 by Debora Jackson
All rights reserved.

Judson Press has made every effort to trace the ownership of all quotes. In the event of a question arising from the use of a quote, we regret any error made and will be pleased to make the necessary correction in future printings and editions of this book.

Scripture quotations are from the New Revised Standard Version of the Bible, copyright © 1989 by the Division of Christian Education of the National Council of the Churches of Christ in the United States of America. Used by permission. All rights reserved. Other quotations are from *The Holy Bible*, King James Version (KJV), and from HOLY BIBLE, New International Version®, NIV®, copyright © 1973, 1978, 1984, 2011 by Biblica Inc. Used by permission. All rights reserved worldwide (NIV).

Interior and cover design by Wendy Ronga, Hampton Design Group.

Library of Congress Cataloging-in-Publication Data
Names: Jackson, Debora, author. Title: Meant for good: fundamentals of womanist leadership / Debora Jackson. Description: Valley Forge, PA : Judson Press, 2020. | Includes index. | Summary: "African American women have survived nearly 400 years of oppression by crafting a culture of resistance, perseverance in the struggle, and the ability to adapt while remaining undergirded by faith. Using the biblical story of Joseph's exile and rise to power in Egypt, author and pastor Debora Jackson highlights leadership fundamentals gleaned from that story and from the stories of black women's experiences that may be redeemed for the good of ourselves and our organizations"—Provided by publisher.
Identifiers: LCCN 2019045835 (print) | LCCN 2019045836 (ebook) | ISBN 9780817018108 (paperback) | ISBN 9780817082093 (ebook) Subjects: LCSH: Womanist theology. | Leadership—Religious aspects—Christianity. | Joseph (Son of Jacob) | African American women. Classification: LCC BT83.9 .J33 2020 (print) | LCC BT83.9 (ebook) | DDC 253.082—dc23
LC record available at https://lccn.loc.gov/2019045835
LC ebook record available at https://lccn.loc.gov/2019045836

Printed in the U.S.A.
First printing, 2019.

Contents

The World Needs Our Womanist Light!

Several years ago, my college magazine interviewed me for an article about women's leadership styles. I was chosen because I was somewhat unique; I represented a bit of a throwback to an older model of college leadership—professors who were both pastors and academics. The interviewer asked me how my experience as a college professor shaped my leadership in the church. At that moment I recognized it was my lifelong experiences in *church* that had shaped my leadership in academia. Many of those opportunities to learn, serve, and lead were guided and engineered by the women in our churches. Alice Walker observed these women were "head-ragged generals," opening doors and making pathways even when they did not know the ways themselves. Even my willingness to attend meetings had been formed by the importance of such gatherings in Baptist church life: meetings of the choir, Sunday school, junior usher board, as well as quarterly business meetings and biennial conventions.

Because I learned early in life that showing up at meetings provided a level of knowledge that could be a source of power, I showed up at all-college faculty meetings even when my colleagues had given up on participating. Being black, visible, and present led to access to the overlife and underlife of my institutions of higher education, often placing me in "the room where it happens."

The womanist idea, first offered by Alice Walker, is a concept grounded in the experiences of black women and the cultural sensibilities they have developed to benefit their entire community. Although Walker is an admitted pagan, her insistence that a "womanist *loves* the Spirit" has enabled black women to engage one another across a wide variety of religious and generational differences. Such sharing has nurtured traditions of transformative leadership that are rightly called *womanist.*

Foreword

Rev. Dr. Debora Jackson has taken her experiences as a business leader, engineer, and minister of the gospel and wedded them to the intergenerational stories shared across the kitchen tables of her childhood to provide a theory of leadership that is humane, inclusive, nurturing, and necessary for times like these. Black women in America have generated survival capital and healing strategies to nurture families and communities of faith from the hush harbors of slavery to the historically black churches and community organizations. They have fostered the uplift of an entire people—and have also changed and benefited an entire nation.

Unfortunately, the traps of racism and sexism have limited the ability of black women to occupy positions of leadership, at times even within their communities and churches. Dr. Jackson highlights how black women's distinctive leadership gifts have been used against them to justify exclusionary practices. Rejection and exploitation of black women's differences have fostered cultures of misogyny and racism, which contribute to the anatomy of human destructiveness.

From the example of her own grandmother to that of prominent women such as Anna Julia Cooper and Dorothy Height, Dr. Jackson explores transformative models of leadership that are clearly womanist. Then she challenges us to consider, "What would our organizations look like if more leaders operated in such ways?"

In 1896, Josephine St. Pierre Ruffin said of the women's movement for black women, "We are neither alienating nor withdrawing," but "coming to the front" to share their gifts of leadership. Dr. Jackson has come to the front to assert black women's leadership is "meant for good" for all people. Everyone who cares about a just, equitable, and inclusive society needs to read this book, for inspiration *and* to discover a transformative tradition of womanist leadership, available for "the healing of the nations."

—Cheryl Townsend Gilkes, PhD
John D. and Catherine T. MacArthur Professor of Sociology
and African-American Studies, Colby College
Assistant Pastor, Union Baptist Church,
Cambridge, Massachusetts

Acknowledgments

I thank God for the inspiration that has resulted in this book. I remain humbled for the gifts of word and leadership that God has deposited in me and the opportunity to share these gifts with you.

I thank God for the many people who have been a part of this work, each of whom have helped me bring this book one step closer to fruition. Thank you to the Boston Ministers Club, the oldest continuously functioning ministers' club in the country, through which I had the opportunity to write the first chapter from which this book was birthed. Thank you to my dear sister Rev. Laura Everett, who, having heard my reading at the Boston Ministers Club, was moved to connect me with Sally Hicks, Editor of Duke Divinity School's Faith & Leadership. And thank you Sally Hicks, for the editorial expertise that led to the article, "How my grandmother's story helped me lead as an African-American woman." Of course, I am so grateful to my editor, Rebecca Irwin-Diehl, and the staff of Judson Press. Your excitement about this work constantly motivated me to press on and I thank you for it.

I thank the women of the South Middlesex County Alumnae Chapter of Delta Sigma Theta Sorority, Inc., who cheered and encouraged me throughout the process. Thank you to Rev. Valerie Miles-Tribble, PhD, and Dean LeAnn Snow Flesher, PhD, of American Baptist Seminary of the West, for providing me with the opportunity to serve as Adjunct Faculty where my vision for this work continued to emerge. I am grateful for Christine Kobza and Emily Perlow of Worcester Polytechnic Institute who co-sponsored the event Lessons in Leadership, where I had the privilege of sharing my research and presenting with amazing sisters Roxann Cooke, Dr. Beverly Edgehill, Michelle Jones Johnson, and Dean Jean King, PhD—all strong womanist leaders in their own right. Thanks also to Rev. Martha Simmons,

Acknowledgments

PhD, creator of the Women of Color in Ministry Project, for allowing me to present my findings to a national audience.

Thank you to Danielle Walker and Eberardo Bahena of Image360 in Tucker, Georgia, for your vision and insight in designing the Model of Womanist Leadership graphic. It is a thing of beauty.

Finally, I want to thank my family. To my husband, James Thomas, I am so grateful for your love and support. You lift me up. To our son, Jadon Theodore Thomas, you are my inspiration. To my father, Theodore Jackson, thank you for being my solid rock. And to my mother, Carolyn Jackson, you are the womanist leader whose shining example I follow. Pardon my blackness, but I meant to shine because of what my Momma gave me. I love you all.

Introduction

How do I begin to craft a narrative of womanist leadership, one that commends as good the leadership abilities of African American women? Believing that such a narrative is noteworthy and of value, I could tell a story that is in part autobiographical. I first began formally supervising engineers at the wizened age of twenty-six. Since that time, I have led hundreds of people and dozens of organizations in both for-profit and nonprofit settings. And I would be the first to note that my experiences in leadership have most definitely been shaped by the fact that I am an African American woman. I learned very early, particularly in male-dominated fields, that I could not lead like my peers who were most often white men because I was received differently than they were. These experiences taught me how to be a different kind of leader, and I believe that articulating those differences is important in developing an expanded understanding of how one leads.

I could craft the narrative declaring that the story of African American women in leadership is untold but is yearning to be told. Various academic and psychosocial strands of endeavor have codified epistemological theories to articulate the significance of the African American woman's experience. For example, black feminist liberation theology and womanism shape theological discourse by recognizing that as a double minority, the experiences of African American women are not fully captured in liberation or feminist theology. This recognition has given way to a rapidly growing body of scholarship that speaks to the unique contributions of African American women in various spectrums of education and the sciences.

The same is not true when we speak of leadership. Certainly, there are numerous theories regarding leadership. We can learn how to be a transactional leader, servant leader, adaptive leader, or transformational leader. However, the basis of each of these theories holds as constant a specific focus group as central. These theories have been developed based largely on the experiences of European-descended men. Where theories based on female leadership traits have been developed, they have been based on the European-descended women from a middle-class socioeconomic perspective. The lessons that can be learned from the ways of leading while African American and female have yet to be articulated.

These are motivating factors, but there is more that moves me than simply telling a story, be it autobiographical or untold. It is also the desire to meet an overwhelming need in our communities, which includes our churches and organizations. Our churches and organizations are struggling as the challenges of leadership continue to increase. Religious institutions are declining and closing as members age and resources dwindle. Organizations, gripped with the anxiety and fear of complex challenges, operate in myopic ways that are often polarizing. Leaders are expected to do more with less, the weight of their decisions looming more critically. Under such stress, it is difficult if not impossible to lead expansively. Instead, leaders tend to resort to ingrained ways of behaving: doing more of the same, acting on impulse, and going it alone.

Thus, I am recommending a different path, and that path draws from the leadership experiences of African American women. Certainly, there would be some who would devalue such a strategy. After all, in so many fields of endeavor, African American women have not broken through that glass ceiling in sufficient numbers to quantify deterministically the validity of their leadership strategies. There are glimpses of hope as some African American women have achieved notable firsts. But it would be hard to argue against the claim that the numbers are too small to draw valid conclusions. Few African American women have penetrated the most senior ranks to head Fortune 500 companies or lead the largest institutions. However, I would argue that seeking this kind of quantitative proof is an example of falling into the same operational trap that hampers leadership innovation. The normative ways of being a leader have been employed for decades by tens of thousands, but these strategies have not guaranteed success. Continuing to look for new gains using the same strategies is a strategy of diminishing returns.

African American women bring something different to the table, and it is this difference that I want to concentrate upon for the benefits of people who lead. As a marginalized minority shunted throughout history to the lowest rungs of the socioeconomic and sociopolitical ladder, African American women have been uniquely prepared for leadership. History suggests that the first ship loaded with Africans arrived in the Virginia colony of Jamestown in 1619. Within a generation of their arrival, peoples of African descent had been declared slaves. And with this title of enslavement began a history of oppression and marginalization whose roots remain firmly embedded in the fabric of our country. While people of color in general have been oppressed in this nation's history, this endemic oppression is seen most readily through the experiences of African American women. Because African American women live under the dual stigma of ethnicity and gender, their voices and opinions have often been silenced through systemic stereotyping based on prejudice. These widespread overt and covert practices have relegated African American women to the margins, indelibly stained by abuse and disenfranchisement.

Yet, I am reminded of the words of Maya Angelou who penned, "You may write me down in history with your bitter, twisted lies, you may trod me in the very dirt but still, like dust, I'll rise."[1] African American women have survived nearly four hundred years of oppression in this country by crafting a culture of resistance, perseverance in the struggle, and the ability to change adaptively while remaining undergirded by faith. The lessons gleaned from that story need to be told because these are lessons that are for the good of our organizations.

In fact, it was the phrase "for good" that would not let me go as I considered this need to write. It comes from Genesis 50:20 (NIV) and was spoken by Joseph, son of Jacob and Rachel, to his brothers: "You intended to harm me, but God intended it for good to accomplish what is now being done, the saving of many lives." Oppression and marginalization are instruments of harm, and these tactics have been used to discredit and disenfranchise African American women. Nevertheless, a way of being and a way of knowing were inculcated in African American women in much the same way as Joseph's trials shaped him. In fact, Joseph's entire narrative can be appropriated to describe the plight of African American women and their preparation for leadership.

In Joseph's story, we learn that Joseph is loved by his father, Jacob, more than any of his other children. Moreover, because Joseph's father openly demonstrated his favor toward him, Joseph's brothers hated him. But it was Joseph's visions that spurred his brothers to conspire against him. In his dreams, Joseph saw himself as greater than his brothers, deified in fact, as the one to whom the celestial bodies bowed. Driven by jealously, Joseph's brothers decided to kill him when the opportunity presented itself. However, in a moment of leniency, they opted instead to sell Joseph. Taking Joseph's robe and dipping it in the blood of a slaughtered goat, they allowed their father to believe that Joseph had been killed, while Joseph was sold far from home.

African folklore and stories of the diaspora have depicted women as similarly beloved. Stories speak of African women as powerful goddesses or even as the Divine Mother who was co-equal with men. The narratives varied, but the attributes were often the same. These women were recognized as being powerful and nurturing. They cared for their families, communities, and the earth. They were smart and capable. They were beautiful, fearless, and determined. These women were recognized for their leadership and for their power.

But in some of the same narratives, these leading women were also envied. They were envied by other women for their strength and beauty. They were envied by men for their independence. And those who envied them sought to subjugate them. Stories of enslavement speak of warring tribes that trapped their rivals, selling men and women to people involved in the slave trade. Women, along with men and children, were stolen from their homes, shackled, and marched for miles to be forcibly boarded upon ships. They were separated from families and those they loved. While all were enslaved, stripped, and dehumanized, women suffered the additional perils of violation and rape. Once envied, these women were relegated to enslavement, just like Joseph.

But God favored Joseph during his enslavement. Despite being a slave of Potiphar, who was the captain of the guard and an officer of Pharaoh, Joseph was blessed by God, such that all that he did prospered. Because Joseph flourished, Potiphar flourished as well. When Joseph was imprisoned on the false charge of attempted rape, God continued to bless Joseph. Not only did Joseph find favor with the chief jailer, but also all that was in Joseph's care did well. These leadership roles gave Joseph the opportunity to come before Pharaoh's officials and interpret their dreams. Although two years passed, Joseph's ability to interpret dreams was remembered by Pharaoh's chief cupbearer, which created the opportunity for Joseph to interpret the dreams of Pharaoh. God blessed Joseph, providing him with the vision to see the impending doom of famine. This foreknowledge allowed Joseph to propose a strategy to preserve produce, yielding reserves for the seven years of famine that would occur. His proposal so pleased Pharaoh that he appointed Joseph over all the land of Egypt.

Joseph's story was ultimately a good news narrative from enslavement to leadership, enabled by the grace of God. Again, we see parallels between his narrative and that of African American women. African American women were forced to serve. Women worked in the fields, carrying loads as great as any man. They worked in the houses, cooking, cleaning, caring for the household and all who were in it. They were raped and beaten. They were abused and mistreated. But through it all, God remained. Some suggest that Africans were taught about God in America, but they came already believing in God. They came with a deeply rooted sense of spirituality and connectedness to the land, to one another, and to an omnipresent spirit that united all things. And as they gained language to allow them to articulate the biblical stories of the God of Abraham and Sarah and Hagar, they received that God as their own. They heard the exodus narrative and recognized themselves as the enslaved children of Israel. They heard about the suffering servant Jesus Christ and saw him as their liberator. They held on to this faith in God and were favored. They survived.

In addition, they learned how to care for all that was given into their hands. African American women ran households, directing other enslaved staff in managing the master's house. They learned to take the leftovers from the master's table to make the southern cuisine that is renowned even today. These women took scraps of cloth to make clothing and bedding. And often, when the men were sold away, they filled the void, functioning as heads of households. In short, African American women mastered their domains even as they were being mastered. They learned to lead, and in doing so these African American women persevered for themselves while teaching others to do the same.

Good leadership can save. This is what African American women learned, and Joseph learned this lesson as well. As Egypt plunged into the season of famine, Joseph's leadership saved the nation. But Joseph's leadership also saved people from other nations as they learned that there was food in Egypt. This is how Joseph's brothers were reunited with him. They had to come to him—to bow to him—that they might be saved from famine. Ultimately Joseph brought his entire family, seventy of his kinspeople, to settle in the land of Goshen where they could live and flourish. After Joseph's father, Jacob, died, Joseph's brothers feared that he might hold a grudge for the wrong that they had inflicted upon him. But Joseph reassured his brothers saying that although they meant to harm him, God meant the trials for good that a nation would be saved.

I believe the same to be true for African American women. Through the experiences of slavery, African American women developed a character of perseverance that was rooted in faith and extended to the communities for which they cared. Those characteristics were further sharpened in the early twentieth century and the civil rights era when negative and positive experiences shaped generations of African American women. The result was hard-wrought lessons that were internalized by African American women in the struggle and then imprinted on subsequent generations.

Joseph forgave his brothers because he recognized God's intent to use him to save a people. I would maintain that African American women have come to similarly understand their role in society. Just as their ancestors weaved colorful quilts from the scraps given, African American women have woven communities of care and created an inclusive body oriented toward the determined success of the whole. This is what truly motivates me. As we glean the lessons of the African American women's experience, I believe that we will find pearls of wisdom that have the power to change how organizations lead. African American women have had to learn ways of being and leading to lift themselves and their communities. Through their experiences, they have internalized values of faith, education, advocacy, and service which have led to flourishing in their communities. These are lessons and values that I believe can be communicated. As we understand how African American women have managed to thrive, cultivate, and pass on these strong leadership skills across the generations and in community, we see an enduring, adaptive capacity that is urgently needed in leadership. That is the focus of this book.

Chapter 1 begins to expound upon why such a book is needed. As an African American woman, I observe "My Stories Aren't in the Book" on leadership. The volumes of information on leadership are legion, and many of the terms that are shorthand for popular theories are well-known. However, these strategies have largely been written from the European patriarchal perspective. Even when the focus is strategies for women in leadership, all women are lumped together assuming a Eurocentric model. The ways that African American women have traditionally learned leadership would not be considered leadership in most spheres, but these are the ways of leadership that

I want to highlight. African American women learned leadership from their mothers, grandmothers, and other mothers during daily life. These were the lessons learned at mothers' knees or as women chatted over kitchen chores. Not only was the "mother wit" important, but also how they learned—in silent observation. The lessons and the ways of learning the lessons are what shaped subsequent generations of women. Thus, African American women learned ways of leadership through stories, experiences, observation, and listening. What if we as leaders learned to observe and listen? How might our organizations change if we assessed our environments based on hearing from others? This way of leadership for African American women is a way influenced by the concept of womanism, a term first coined by author Alice Walker. Womanism seeks to be inclusive of issues for women of color, specifically race and class-based oppression, and is committed to survival and the wholeness of the entire people, male *and* female. It is a way of being that African American women embodied through slavery and into the Industrial Revolution, caring for diverse communities of children. This way of being is so embedded that it is a feature of the leadership style of African American women.

Chapter 2, "Use What Your Momma Gave You," speaks of the negative stigmas that African American women have had to endure regarding their bodies. Through history in the United States, African American women have often been subjected to stereotypical labels meant to demean, marginalize, or rationalize abuse. Saartjie Baartman, unfortunately known as the Hottentot Venus, epitomized such stereotyping. Her physical appearance was used to reinforce sexualized stereotypes associated with African American women, who were said to be bestial and sexually deviant. Such labeling was used during days of enslavement to justify rape, as African American women were said to want or need sex. The labels persist to the present time, and even when thinly veiled, the intent to apply them for marginalization remains. However, African American women have learned to reclaim a sense of celebration and joy in what their mommas gave them. Recognizing the dignity that comes from the affirmation that they are made in God's image, African American women have declared their goodness and self-worth. Moreover, they have learned to subvert the use of negative labels for positive ends. The stereotypical caricatures that were identified to demean women were the ones that changeably functioned to accomplish the task at hand. Acknowledging themselves as fearfully and wonderfully made,[2] African American women have donned a self-aware confidence which helps them extend that confidence to others.

As Psalm 27:1 declares that the Lord is the strength of my life, an exploration of leadership for African American women must be focused in the faith. Chapter 3, "If It Had Not Been for the Lord on My Side," provides that focus. Church and matters of faith remain bedrock in the black community in the twenty-first century with nearly 80 percent of African Americans self-identifying as Christians, according to the Pew Research Center.[3] The predominance of women in the church and the importance of religion in the African American community doubly underscore the importance of religion and matters of faith for African American women.

Faith is central to the personhood of African American women. In fact, African American women have been the backbone of the black church for centuries. These are the churches comprised primarily from the historical African American denominations in the United States, and in them, African American women have remained faithful even as generations of people fall away from the church and religious practice. Historically, African American churches were formed by people who refused continued segregation in worship. Tiring of being relegated to balconies or the back of the sanctuaries, they wanted the freedom to worship and established churches where that exercise of freedom could occur. So, it seems that people who railed for freedom would recognize the same desires of women who wanted the freedom to lead as God has called. But that has not been the case. The same churches and pastors who refute Scripture-based discriminatory practices based on race or ethnicity uphold the biblical authority of Scripture that discriminates based on gender. Yet women continue to devote themselves in service and participation in the church. Why is this, especially given the sexist practices of the black church?

Chapter 3 explains why. African American women are the most religiously devout, but additionally, the church has been a place of formation for women. With the church dominated by women, so much of what the church offers is for women. And from these formational opportunities, women have carved places from which to lead in formal and informal ways, from the various auxiliaries, ministries, and increasingly, the pulpit. Driven by a faith in God that asserts their giftedness, African American women have used faith to shape their beliefs in the call of leadership. But also, faith drives their mandate to care for others as leaders. Rooted in faith in God by Jesus Christ, African American women exhibit their faith through service.

People of color in general and African America women specifically will speak of having to be the smartest persons in the group to be recognized as having any valid opinion. Chapter 4, "Pardon My Blackness, I Didn't Mean to Shine," speaks to this reality. It is a saying from my formative years, and it speaks of overcoming stereotypes that are meant to marginalize. To identify an African American as a "shine" is a racial slur with origins that are hundreds of years old. But African American students of my parents' generation inverted the meaning to turn it into a compliment about academic excellence. Such affirmations were needed because, as African American parents and grandparents taught their children, you must be twice as good as others to get half as far. African American women heard these words and took them to heart, shouldering the responsibilities for education. Discrimination was so endemic that race served as a disqualifier by a dominant culture. Lacking education, African Americans were confined to low-wage job opportunities where they were regularly exploited. Thus, African American leaders embraced the philosophy of racial uplift.[4] According to educator Jeanne Noble, there was a general attitude that "Negro women should be trained to teach in order to uplift the masses."[5] African American women created educational opportunities for their children and communities by starting schools. Lucy C. Laney founded a school for children in Augusta, Georgia, in 1883. Nannie Helen Burroughs established the National Training School for women in 1908. Mary McLeod Bethune founded the Educational and Industrial Training School for Negro Girls in 1904. These schools provided an academic curriculum, but they also taught respectability in the home and in the belief that if all African Americans would exercise a level of decorum, they would be deemed acceptable by white society. Burroughs's National Training School taught domestic services so that women employed as domestics could better advocate for themselves. As women raised their profile, they lifted others, and continuing this legacy of education, African American women are among the most educated people in the country. According to the National Center for Educational Statistics, 64 percent of associate's and bachelor's degrees conferred between the academic years 2000–2001 and 2015–2016 were awarded to African American women.[6]

But the challenge for African American women is that being twice as good creates other challenges. African American women are often viewed as threatening or intimidating. The number of single African American professional women continues to grow as women with higher levels of academic achievement or professional advancement struggle to find marriage partners. Additionally, leadership traits that are viewed positively in men, such as assertiveness, certainty, or intelligence, are viewed as aggressiveness, bossiness, or boastfulness in women. Certainly, women of all races suffer from being discounted, complaining that their comments are not acknowledged until male colleagues offer the same insights, at which time the ideas are heralded. However, in response, many African American women speak of engaging defense mechanisms that mask their true feelings. They hide behind a persona, remaining seemingly impervious to marginalizing or critical responses. Yet, given this posture, African American women have learned to assess situations to draw conclusions or steel themselves against hurtful reactions for self-preservation and protection. Such strategies have enabled African American women to shrewdly navigate social systems by deftly using their intelligence in ways that have helped them to shine.

However, the efforts of African American women have been more generative, inclusive, and rooted in community, as was taught in African culture. This view of African American women in community is the focus of chapter 5, "All God's Children Got Shoes." The Negro spiritual of the same title spoke of an aspirational time. Harkening to the days of enslavement and reconstruction, the song described people who did not have shoes to cover their feet. But one day, everyone would have all that was needed, if not in this life, then in the life to come. In that day, all of God's children would have shoes.

But where enslaved people were told to wait until reaching their heavenly reward to realize all that was needed, African American women have worked so that the needs of the community would be met in the present day. Through their communal efforts, African American women have developed a model for leadership that promotes development at the local community level, extending their learning to subsequent generations. For example, African American women demonstrate a leadership model that meets people where they are and empowers group decision making by encouraging small-group interaction rather than hierarchical leadership. African American women also lead in community by encouraging people to engage in the day-to-day, gritty work of advocacy. This strategy directly translates to the ways that African American women train children because they instill in them a communal and cooperative work responsibility, assigning age-appropriate chores. As children mature, these communal tasks help them to see themselves in community while creating a sense of pride through task accomplishment.

Each of these chapters speaks of ways of being that are part of the fabric of the African American woman's experience. However, it is more than just a way of being. It is an instructive and innovative way of leading an organization. Self-defined and adaptive, rooted in faith, shrewdly wise in relationships, and generatively inclusive are traits offered throughout the chapters to reinforce core ways of being and leading for African American women. Chapter 6, "Then My Living Will Not Be in Vain," brings these characteristics together in sharp focus by offering a model of womanist leadership that demonstrates how these lessons may be employed in the broader community. It is a model that can transform communities, be those communities a local congregation or an organization, because it encourages leaders to orient themselves to serve, as they are rooted in faith, expanded in their perspectives, and girded by strategies that encourage. This model helps leaders to build accountable, caring organizations that bring forth the best of individuals and adapt to meet confronting challenges.

I believe that God means these experiences for the good, that people are helped and organizations are transformed as they become aware and mindful of the stories that can make a difference in leadership. These are personal stories, undervalued in the context of leadership. These are stories of faith, shaped in the crucible of marginalization and oppression but indicative of perseverance. The stories of African American women and their experiences have uniquely positioned them to lead. And believing that the stories are not only communicable but also beneficial in helping communities, congregations, and organizations innovatively reorient their ways of being so that they are able to make progress on confronting challenges, I am moved to share these lessons in womanist leadership for good.

Notes

1. "Still I Rise," from *And Still I Rise: A Book of Poems* by Maya Angelou, copyright © 1978 by Maya Angelou. Used by permission of Random House, an imprint and division of Penguin Random House LLC. All rights reserved.

2. Psalm 139:14.

3. David Masci, "Five Facts about the Religious Lives of African Americans," Pew Research Center, February 7, 2018, https://www.pewresearch.org/fact-tank/2018/02/07/5-facts-about-the-religious-lives-of-african-americans/, accessed May 30, 2019.

4. Racial uplift is the philosophy that educated or middle-class African Americans were responsible for using their education, influence, and means to lift others who were less able or capable. Educators such as Booker T. Washington and W. E. B. DuBois were prominent proponents, but African American women of the early twentieth century such as Mary Church Terrell, Lucy Laney, and Nannie Helen Burroughs took this philosophy to heart as well as they worked to establish schools.

5. Paula Giddings, *When and Where I Enter: The Impact of Black Women on Race and Sex in America* (New York: HarperCollins, 1984), 101.

6. National Center for Education Statistics, Fast Facts: Degrees Conferred by Race and Sex, https://nces.ed.gov/fastfacts/display.asp?id=72, accessed June 12, 2019.

CHAPTER 1

My Stories Aren't in the Book

It was the 1950s.[1] My grandmother, Edith Jackson, was shopping in downtown Elkhart, Indiana, and as she passed a department store window, the display stopped her in her tracks. A lovely white woman was posing next to a brand-new washing machine. Next to this was a mechanized, fat, black woman with a bandana on her head, reminiscent of Aunt Jemima, laboring over an old-fashioned scrub board. This image incensed my grandmother, and she marched into the store, demanding to see the store manager.

"You take that display down," she insisted of the manager. "We wash our clothes just like everybody else; you take that down!"

She declared that she would complete her shopping, but upon her return, she expected the display to be removed. With that pronouncement, she turned on her heel and marched out of the store.

Understand that my grandmother was 4' 10" tall and hardly 100 pounds. She would not have intimidated anyone based on her stature. Moreover, people in an overwhelmingly white, Midwestern city in conservative Indiana would have hardly felt pressed to comply with the demands of an angry, African American woman. So, it was not surprising that the store manager waved off my grandmother's threat with hardly a second thought. Of course, that was before she returned.

Seeing that the display was unmoved, my grandmother took matters into her own hands. She climbed into the display window and, using her oversized pocketbook, as it was called in those days, proceeded to knock down the entire display. Angered, the store manager promptly called police, but my grandmother firmly stood her ground as she waited their arrival.

"Edith," the police officer said to her. "You know you can't be doing things like this."

"Well, they can't be telling lies like this either," my grandmother huffed. "We wash our clothes like everybody else."

I never knew my grandmother. She died before I was born. So, how did I come to learn of this exchange? This was just one of the stories that was told at the kitchen table when the family got together. These were the stories that the women told as they snapped beans, shelled peas, or picked greens. These were the stories that little girls heard as their hair was braided while they sat between their mother's knees. And I remember that when I heard the stories, they were often comical in the retelling, but the wisdom, passion, and assertion of personhood were not laughed away. These were the stories that shaped us, and as we plumbed the depths of the stories, we realized that our leadership narrative was handed down to us through them. For example, I learned of a paternal grandmother with a strong spirit, sense of justice, and powerful voice whose legacy was imprinted on her children and as such passed to me. And because of the stories that were passed down, I gained a newfound sensitivity regarding how I lead as an African American woman. It differs significantly from what I was taught formally in a business school degree program.

We live in a society where the dominant culture is given the latitude to shape what is deemed normative, and our definition of who and what makes a good leader fits into that norm. For example, popular culture of the 1940s and 1950s provided us with the enduring leadership model of John Wayne, which remains persistent today. John Wayne, a 6' 4" tall white man, with looks that featured a chiseled jawline, was the epitome of leadership strength. His commanding voice and dimpled chin suggested character. His piercing blue eyes were a sign of clarity and certainty. When he barked out commands, of course you rallied to do what he said to do.

Yes, this was Hollywood's sign of leadership, but it seemed to be a standard norm in our business environments as well. From the "great man" theory of leadership, theorists espoused that leadership was about embodying certain characteristics which could not be taught. Such leaders had a defined set of qualities that seemingly set them apart as having endowed powers. Such abilities were thought to be innate and were recognized especially during times of great challenge. These were larger-than-life leaders who were ruggedly individualistic and heroic. Such a leader was the Lone Ranger, the fictionalized Western hero who fought outlaws in the old American West. Self-made and answering to no one, this leader was also charismatic, certain, and decisive. These traits engendered a following. Intelligence kept them one step ahead, and it instilled confidence in the leader's know-how.

This model of leadership, rooted not only in the "old West" of Hollywood but also in western, patriarchal culture, gives preference to traits that are "rational, management oriented, male, technocratic, quantitative, goal dominated, cost-benefit driven, personalistic, hierarchical, short term, pragmatic, and materialistic."[2] And because this model of leadership was successful in so many spheres, these styles were replicated across varying industries. I have watched male pastors, for example, function in ways similar to those of Fortune 500 company leaders. While the congregation would largely eschew the idea of functioning as a corporation, church members also want the westernized normative leader because of the confidence that leader instills. Although the "great man" leadership model has receded in importance to other theories of leadership, it continues to shape leadership practice because society continues to look for that "great man" to lead. We have been acculturated to follow larger-than-life figures. Such leaders—typically male—can project a self-assured certainty that rules the day and garners a following. From this perspective, effectiveness in leadership is measured by people with these preferred traits who are also able to influence followers to do what the leader wishes.

Well, guess what? I am a 5' 1½" African American woman. I do not have a chiseled jawline; my dark brown eyes would never be mistaken for blue. When I bark out commands, people assume that

I am the characteristically angry black woman. There is nothing about the John Wayne personification that I can embody. And I can distinctly remember times in my career when my lacking that embodiment was an issue.

I was a software engineering supervisor working for an organization that developed software systems to test computers during the manufacturing process. Newly minted as a supervisor, I went to meet, one on one, with one of my engineers: an employee who fit the engineer stereotype to a T. He was a grizzled, older white man who made his home an office cubicle stacked high with computer manuals, dirty coffee cups, and empty fast-food wrappers. He arrived at the office early and stayed late into the evening, leaving his cubicle only to use the bathroom. I was intimidated by having him as a direct report because he was a principal-level engineer with decades of experience. I had just received my master of engineering management degree and had less than five years of experience. What value could I add to him as his supervisor?

Clearly, he had the same question when I entered his office for the first time with this new reporting relationship. He raised his head above his computer screen and stated baldly, "I don't need a supervisor," and returned to his work. From his perspective, I brought no value to the table. While I did not know what characteristics he believed to be of value, I knew the traits of my predecessor supervisors. They were all white men who had risen to the ranks of principal engineer prior to becoming supervisors. They were known for their technical prowess: engineers who had distinguished themselves developing complex pieces of code that accomplished transformative work in this rapidly growing industry. They had climbed the ranks in the manufacturing plants and were said to have solder paste under their fingernails. They knew how to read the multileveled layers of circuit boards and were well-studied in hexadecimal coding languages. I had none of those capabilities, and if that was the measuring stick against which I was regarded, this engineer was correct; he did not need a supervisor, or more specifically, he did not need me.

4

However, this is the point: my stories are not in the classic leadership book because my profile was never considered as plausible or valuable. The fitting profile was based on a male-dominated, Eurocentric, and economically advantaged framework that could be leveraged to produce and champion highly skilled knowledge workers. In this environment, one needed to have significant seasoning and credentialing. I did not have it. This environment prized masculine tendencies such as hierarchy, autonomy, control, unilateralism, and aggressiveness. I could not do it. I did not fit the profile.

Naïvely, I believed that I could rectify the situation through education. Although I earned a master's degree in a program specifically designed for technical leaders, I returned to school for further studies, earning a master of engineering in manufacturing engineering with a minor in computer science. Now, no one could say that I did not have the technical credentials. That credentialing demonstrated that I could be technical, rational, and quantitative in my approach. But I still lacked critical components. I was not white, and I was not a man. Because of that, I was regularly discounted in my leadership roles. Plant workers in Puerto Rico refused to pose their questions to me, even though I was the project leader. Engineers on the manufacturing floor in Scotland stared at me as though I had made a wrong turn seeking the secretarial pool when I walked onto the manufacturing floor to implement process changes. I could not tour the manufacturing plant in Ontario that was producing my product because they did not have anti-static grounding straps to fit my pumps.

Furthermore, as I sought to find my leadership place, what were deemed as the markers of female leadership were also ill-fitting. The leadership profiles that came into vogue in the 1960s and 1970s encouraged women to emulate men and their leadership style. The only female supervisor in our organization clearly heeded these recommendations. Being viewed as one of the guys was the strategy she executed for acceptance. It was a strategy that worked for many women. These were the women who would climb under computers to connect cables, get dirty on the manufacturing line, or engage in the true manufacturing rite of passage at the end of the day: pub crawling. I too learned to "mind my pints and quarts" with my male manufacturing colleagues. However, at issue was that I did not want to shed my femininity at the door just to fit in. I was not interested in some of the gritty, grimy work of the manufacturing floor, nor was I interested in earning a badge of honor by being one of the boys. I was a leader who happened to be female, and I wanted to live authentically into my own sense of what it meant to lead.

So, if functioning as a quasi-male leader model did not fit, what about functioning in what were said to be female leadership styles? Viewed from the perspective of stereotypically gendered roles, female leadership styles were touted as the soft skills. Women were more qualitative in their dealings. And given such a qualitative focus, it was suggested that women in leadership should operate in more participatory ways. With styles supposedly grounded in female values, women were encouraged to gravitate toward a passive, nurturing, relationship-oriented leadership style.[3] Relationship building and interdependence were said to be chief areas of functioning for women.

In *Female Advantage*, Sally Helgesen posited that females, who value cooperation and relationship over complex rules and authoritarian structures,[4] have skill in building web-based relationships. Such feminine styles of leadership were suggested to make women better leaders than men because these feminine styles were more suited for the complexities of contemporary organizations.[5] Her ideas were developed in the crucible of high-task, high-complexity environments that benefited from diverse perspectives and viewpoints. Information needed to move rapidly, and varying points of view needed to be shared widely to realize effectiveness in such environments. Women tended to create organizations that fit this model of functioning because women-led organizations were characterized by a network or web of relationships with leadership at the center. The relational nature of such organizations maximized information flow and sharing. Additionally, such organizations fostered principles of caring and intuitive creativity because others were brought into the decision-making process through the web of relations.

Certainly, as a woman, I appreciated some of these styles. I found it useful to promote the concept of team, focusing on relationship building as the core strategy. I would also credit this focus on my successes in ministry because I was able to build strong followings and support through my relationships. Creating interconnected networks of people based on strong relationships was far more effective in my career than creating the hierarchy that was inherently suggested in the standard leadership curriculum. Through teamwork, my teams succeeded in solving confronting challenges, because teamwork encouraged greater diversity of thought and receptivity to unique ideas. So, I unapologetically used styles that would be considered characteristically female as primary leadership strategies.

But still, something was missing. Some of the styles fit, but often, they were unnuanced. For example, my tendency to lead as I built community was not rooted in the idea that it was a workable strategy or good thing to do. My motivation was more culturally grounded. I remember, for example, the elderly women who cared for the neighborhood children during the day, ensuring that we got to school in the mornings and had a safe place to return at the end of the school day. Not only did such women provide care, but also they made it possible for mothers to work outside of the home to make ends meet. This culture of care was enabling for the children and for the families who were supported. As a leader, I was unwittingly attempting to create community because that was my cultural indoctrination. So, the use of the relational leadership style fit, but the motivation for using it was not as espoused in any of the leadership training in which I was engaged.

The same could be said for other characteristically female leadership styles. There might have been common application in using a style, but the motivation or rationale for use was often more nuanced and therefore less reflective of me as a leader. Patricia S. Parker argues "that the prevailing vision of feminist leadership is one that reinforces symbolic images of White, middle-class American women."[6] In other words, the same shortcomings that characterize what was purported to be good or effective leadership, a westernized, male-centric model, plagued the characteristics of female leadership. The leadership styles and traits that were lifted as defining markers were the defining markers of a dominant cultural, gender-specific subset.

Moreover, white women have struggled with embodying these feminine leadership characteristics as well. Competing masculine and feminine leadership styles often create an unworkable dichotomy for women. Women who were expected to function in stereotypical ways for women also needed the ability to don dominant masculine traits such as rationality, confidence, and strength in their leadership styles. I have heard women speak of needing to function with an iron fist covered by a velvet glove. Women had to be hard and tough as needed, but that toughness had to be meted out with a soft touch. The implicit expectation for women in leadership was clear: you must be able to be both male and female in leadership. And you had to be both even when organizational challenges seemed to recommend feminine styles over masculine ones.

Additionally, stereotypically masculine characteristics were more positively regarded. Male styles, which were said to initiate structure and be task-oriented, focused on performance and the achievement of organizational goals, because men were regarded "as instrumental, competent, rational and assertive."[7] These traits were compared with those of women: sensitive, warm, tactful, and expressive. At issue was that male-oriented traits were judged as superior to female-oriented traits in comparison. Thus, a woman's leadership style was regarded as a lesser substitute. Moreover, such comparisons revealed an unarticulated bias. If a woman's way of leading is seen as lesser than that of a man, and that way of leading is seen as suboptimal even when the organizational dynamics call for more participatory ways of leading, is it possible for women to be positively received, particularly at senior levels of leadership? Moreover, what does this bias mean for those who are not white men or women?

It is this point that resonated with me as I attempted to find expression in the unique ways that I led as an African American woman. To that end, I was particularly captured by the words of

Sandra Harding, who argued that "androcentric, economically advantaged, racist, Eurocentric, and heterosexist conceptual frameworks [continue to ensure] systematic ignorance and error about not only the lives of the oppressed, but also the lives of the oppressors and thus about how nature and social relations in general work."[8] In other words, the framework and theories which defined leadership and how they are best exercised for maximum effectiveness remain at their foundation male-dominated. Additionally, the preference for these theories ensured a continued ignorance regarding how others lead because that perspective is not valued. As a result, social relations are affected because the voices of the other become muted as they are disregarded.

But more than that, because of a general ignorance about aspects of leadership for people in the minority, resources to confront unique challenges that minorities face do not exist. For example, I remember trying to sternly address my team, rallying us to meet an important deadline but also demonstrating that I was serious and needed to be taken as such. I tried valiantly to balance the right levels of charism, certainty, and assertiveness in leading because this is purportedly what strong leaders do. But in response, one of my engineers laughed, saying, "You're cute when you're angry." Because of experiences as both an African American and a woman, it was difficult to know how to process the comment or know how to react in response. Was it racist, sexist, or both? The remark was sexist, but it was also racist and rooted in the racialized history of this country because white men are known to feel particularly emboldened when interacting with black women. The legacy of slavery in the United States, coupled with a level of ignorance that results from white privilege, served to normalizes such comments. Therefore, this engineer thought nothing of referring to me, his supervisor, as cute when angry. Yet, had I responded out of my indignation, I would have been labeled "hypersensitive" and "too easily offended." Where was the curriculum that would help me as an African American woman in leadership deal with such a situation? It did not exist.

Moreover, when I have attempted to be softer and more relational, I have found myself ignored. For example, functioning in highly charged, aggressive meetings, which characterized most engineering environments, a soft approach resulted in invisibility. Was I being paranoid? No; the phenomenon of invisibility regularly plagues African American women. It is the "lack of individuation or differentiation between group members," and it is manifest in situations when black women's faces go unnoticed or poorly recognized, or their voices are misattributed to others, relative to those of white women and black and white men.[9]

A study was conducted with college-aged white participants on predominantly white campuses to determine whether spoken statements made by black women were less likely to be attributed to them as compared with black men, white women, and white men.[10] Participants viewed a discussion between eight targets—two black women, two black men, two white women, and two white men—and were later tested to determine speaker attribution. If the participant was presented with a statement that was heard in the conversation, they were then asked to identify the target speaker.

The results were sobering. In every category, black women were likely to be confused with every other target. Statements made by black women were most likely to be attributed to other speakers. As the researchers concluded, because the black women's statements could be confused between the two black female targets and all others, the theory of invisibility had new credence. But more than invisibility, the study suggested that black women were not unnoticed or unheard but rather were treated as interchangeable and indistinguishable from others and as a result are less visible when compared with other groups.[11]

So, if I cannot fully leverage male leadership strategies; if feminine or feminist strategies do not fully fit; and the uniqueness of my leadership as an African American female leader either renders me a target for racist or sexist remarks or reduces me to invisibility, how am I to function effectively as a leader? It is complicated. I have felt the pressure to be "hard like a man," "soft like a female," and forceful in all instances simply to be noticed. But trying to play all these roles simultaneously does not always work. I was reminded of this as I watched the testimony of Professor Christine Blasey Ford during the hearings for the nomination of Justice Brett Kavanaugh to the Supreme Court. While Professor Ford's testimony was not given full credence, her credibility was enhanced, in part, because of her tearful timidity. But contrast this to hearings in 1991, when Professor Anita Hill alleged that Justice Clarence Thomas sexually harassed her. Professor Hill was assertive, exhibiting a steady, prosecutorial style during her testimony. Tears made Ford credible, but assertiveness made Hill not credible. And this is the rub. An African American woman would not have been able to portray herself as Professor Ford did. She would not have been received. It is a double bind for African American women in leadership—assertiveness can be unwelcome, but passivity is not accepted either.

Additionally, my leadership preference when interacting with others is to be reflective and reserved in deliberations rather than assertive. Some might mistake this style for passivity, but it is part of that complicating affect in leadership as an African American woman. Through observation, I can be discerning, thereby drawing conclusions. However, such a tendency presents a risk that others would see me as apathetic or disengaged. Taking time to reflect is misinterpreted as being detached or uncertain. My leadership confidence or certainty is also questioned if I give too much preference to welcoming input or soliciting diverse opinions. As a result, solicitation must be balanced with strength and capability, so that no one would conclude that I am beyond my depth and clueless.

It is dizzying, but many African American women have learned to lead in these ways because such undocumented strategies were required for survival as leaders. For me personally, I have learned to modulate my emotions and responses based on the situation. As such, I can be soft or hard, passive or assertive, impassively persuasive or energetically convincing. But at the core, I am a community builder and staunch defender, advocating for what is fair and equitable. In fact, it was this aspect of my leadership style that was on display when I lobbied for enhanced equipment and increased compensation for my engineers. And in response, having successfully supplied my team with the equipment needed for our advanced manufacturing work, the gruff and grizzled engineer who declared that he had no use for a supervisor recanted and acknowledged that maybe he needed a supervisor after all. When considered in totality, the theory behind these leadership traits may have been attributable to various male or female leadership styles, but the praxis, how I applied the theory, was unique to who I was as a leader.

Is There a Theory of Leadership for African American Women?

The theory and praxis that characterize how African American women lead remains ill-defined because it continues to be, as I would posit, an undervalued realm of study. African American women are underrepresented in senior leadership ranks across a variety of industries and disciplines. As of 2018, there are no African American women who serve as CEOs of Fortune 500 companies. As of 2013, African American women comprised less than 1 percent of pastors in Baptist churches.[12] Nevertheless, when the experiences of African American women leaders become the focus, what is revealed is a perspective that challenges the either/or dichotomy of male or female leadership models, making space for an informative way of leading based on the unique perspective or standpoint of African American women.

This is the expressed goal of feminist standpoint theory, a system that emerged in the 1970s to situate and understand women as the subject of study through their lived experiences of marginality and oppression. One's standpoint, by definition, is a means of knowing based on that individual's perspective and affirms as valuable the knowledge that is derived from one's social context. Consider, for example, the use of home remedies to cure illnesses. I remember the stories of grandmothers and great-grandmothers who concocted poultices. They developed and administered concoctions based on learned experiences, which is the crux of a standpoint. To disregard that knowledge because it does not adhere to current practices or popular preferences demonstrates prejudice and bias. However, as we assert our standpoint, particularly in response to those who would attempt to minimize the value of individual experiences, we realize an important means of resisting systems of domination.[13] Knowledge gained from the experience of one's individual perspective has value.

Feminist standpoint theory is also a means for gaining an expanded social perspective because the situations of marginalized people make them more aware than non-marginalized people. For example, women understand a situational perspective as a woman but must also understand that same perspective from the male point of view, as male voices are often most dominant. Logic follows that a person of color's standpoint is additionally shaped by the experience of marginalization. From this it becomes clear that a standpoint theory can be identified across marginalizing boundaries, expansively demonstrating that a standpoint theory is not a singular occurrence but numerous in that there are standpoint theories.

These realities make feminist standpoint theory appropriate for the study of African American women and leadership. Too often, African American women have been like the "best friend forever" in a modern-day situational comedy, relegated to the sidelines of the narrative with only tangential coverage because the narratives were largely focused on someone else. This has meant that the experiences of African American women have been lumped into and generalized with those of other women. However, to assert a unique standpoint whose experiences are different from the socialized or dominant norm is a first step in making a counter-hegemonic movement. To say that my experiences are not in the book is to claim the uniqueness of my narrative while also demonstrating an ability to relate to some aspects of narratives defined by the experiences of others.

This is the pioneering work that standpoint theory has the potential to realize. When marginalized groups speak their truths as leaders and how their sense of knowing and being is shaped through their perspectival lenses, new learning can occur. Their experiences, particularly in leadership, are not reduced to selective amalgamations of theories, tactics, and strategies. They are instructive characteristics that unapologetically define unique ways of leading without need for comparison with someone else's story or narrative. Moreover, when these leadership characteristics are considered from the perspective of an African American woman, the inherent complexity of those experiences increases the potential for learning. It was Patricia Hill Collins, in referencing the standpoint theories of African American women, who offered important assertions to this point. Hill noted that African American women are self-defining, autonomously self-determining, and self-valuing, exhibiting a willingness to embrace stereotypical characteristics used to demean.[14] These traits serve to reject negative and controlling, externally defined images. As self-defining, African American women have learned to assert personhood in ways that necessarily defied social convention for the benefit of self, family, and community. Society often countered, employing tactics that attempted to put women in their places and insisting that certain traits or behaviors were unbecoming of women. But being self-valuing, African American women have embraced negative attributions such as assertiveness, for example, if it enables the accomplishment of a necessary task. This kind of self-definition and self-valuation was efficacious because it redefined womanhood while overcoming limiting stereotypes.

Second, consideration of the standpoint of African American women expands our knowledge because it requires the recognition of the linked and interlocking nature of race, gender, and class oppression. This reality is the nature of intersectionality, which denotes the ways in which race, gender, and class interact to shape the multiple dimensions of the African American woman's experiences.[15] Because women of color operate at the nexus of these intersections, ways of being and functioning are inextricably enmeshed and simultaneously confronted in these systems. Am I responding to a social situation as a woman, or racial minority, or as one acquainted with economic challenges? The reality is all these factors come into play and serve as inseparable, distinguishing characteristics that collaborate as I navigate social situations. These factors create a multidimensional view of the world because they account for systemic variables that change how one engages their environment. We see this play out when we acknowledge that African American women have been assigned the inferior half of several dualities—black/white, male/female, economically advantaged/disadvantaged, and so on—which is central to continued domination.[16] When an African American woman advocates for her rights as a person of color, she remains at the mercy of gender-oppressive tactics and vice versa. This is the multiple effect of the pervasive and linked nature of oppressive systems. It is not possible to distinguish independently the drivers of oppression because the systems effectively collaborate to oppress. And the simultaneity of oppressive effects may well make African American women more sensitive to oppressive systems than others. As a result, feminist standpoint theory viewed from the perspective of the African American woman stresses an inclusive stance that demands a holistic analysis of these persistent challenges.

Taken together, the cultural experiences of African American women provide the ideological frame of reference that teaches us how to deal with circumstances and gain for ourselves self-definitions and self-valuations that are essential to navigating the simultaneous impact of multiple oppressions.[17] For example, my leadership style has emerged from the combined appropriation and shedding of dominant cultural styles, enhanced through the application of what was contextually appropriate for me without concern for whether that style was appropriate for others. Thus, through the journey, I have had to understand what it means to lead from a white man's perspective, which provided some insights to male leadership norms. And because my story has been lumped in with that of white women leaders, I have knowledge of their leadership norms. However, by claiming the uniqueness of my leadership style as an African American woman, given those experiences which were at times shaped through the lens of marginalization, I have a fuller view of leadership and am positioned ideally for greater effectiveness. That experience becomes an illuminating means of recognizing in the aggregate how African American women have risen above these systems to survive.

However, this African American female view, which traditionally rests at or near the bottom rung of the societal ladder, is informative, and I believe potentially transformational for our organizations. "The values that have helped black women survive are entirely communicable. And at a time when the problems of our society seem insoluble and the obstacles to peace and freedom insurmountable, all Americans have a great deal to learn from the history of black women in America."[18] By understanding the experiences of African American women and learning from those experiences, aspects of leadership not typically considered rise to the fore because people who have had to operate on the margins are forced to function differently than those who have the benefit of privilege. "The social order looks different from the perspective of our lives and our struggles."[19] It is illustrative to speak of experiences as a woman, but the intersectionality of ethnicity, race, class, and a variety of other factors adds completely different dimensions—different standpoints. This reality is what women of color in general and African American women specifically bring to leadership. The complexities of our situations as women, people of color, and leaders who are serving in privileged yet racialized and sexualized social environments create opportunities for innovation. That innovation is often hard-wrought, but the result, having been proven, are communicable.

Womanist Leadership

I believe that this appreciation for and recognition of the multifaceted and informative experiences, gifts, and abilities of African American women is what womanism seeks to describe. Alice Walker first coined the term "womanism" in her book *In Search of Our Mothers' Gardens*. Her book opens with a complex definition of womanism.[20]

However, several key points stand out in presenting an operable definition. A womanist is a black feminist or feminist of color. Opposite of childish or girlish, a womanist is serious, and at times willful and impudent. A womanist appreciates the gifts and abilities of women and what women uniquely bring to the table. Yet she is not exclusive in that womanists are "committed to [the] survival and wholeness of [an] entire people, male *and* female."[21] This is a designation that distinguishes womanism from feminism. Womanism welcomes men, seeing their inclusion as a vital aspect of humanity's survival. Feminism, in comparison, began as a separatist movement because it largely excluded men. Moreover, feminism was seen traditionally as a white, middle-class women's movement and rarely included women of color.[22] However, inclusivity emboldens womanism, but it does not mean that she cannot be independent. A womanist is traditionally capable, believing in self-efficacy, and loving, particularly of herself.[23]

It is as African American women speak of their leadership perspectives that the hallmarks of womanism emerge. African American women embody womanist values like survival, liberation, wholeness, spirituality, empowerment, family, community, reciprocity, egalitarianism, and extended family. African American women leaders have had to be serious, willful, and at times impudent as leaders. Womanist leaders have come to value their abilities and what makes them unique as leaders. However, the appreciation is not for self-aggrandizement, but instead for the betterment of all. And as this form of leadership has been focused on garnering the gifts and abilities of all, African American women have seen themselves as having the ability to get the job done, whatever that job might be. That is the crux of womanist leadership.

How then does one claim or reclaim the value of leadership from a womanist standpoint? It is from one's stories. More specifically, it is from the stories of the women who have shaped us. As noted, womanism is not gender-exclusive, but it does value and promote the experiences of women. And this is critical in terms of leadership, because what we saw from other women during our formational years may

17

not have been what we recognized or valued as leadership, and as such, we may not recognize these lessons as leadership. I think back to my grandmother and her exercise of indignant civil disobedience. Was she a leader? Absolutely! But neither my father nor his siblings spoke of their mother's role in the narrative as that of a leader. It was simply a narrative that provided insight to the spirit of this indominable woman. Yet, as I relive the narrative, I can also reclaim the valuable nuggets that are indicative of leadership.

My grandmother was a leader because she spoke truth to power. She marched into a store, undaunted by the power imbalance of a man who the dominant culture would have esteemed far more. In her indignation, she demanded justice. She saw an unjust display and insisted that it be deconstructed and removed. When she saw non-compliance, my grandmother was willing to take matters into her own hands, climbing into the display window and using her pocketbook like a battle axe. Even when law enforcement was called to intercede, she refused to back down. Without question, my grandmother was a leader, and from this powerful example of leadership, I can find my voice as a leader, appreciating the unique qualities and characteristics that harken back to those of my grandmother.

Researchers including Naomi Lowinsky gave a name to the generations of women who carry within them the history and biology of a family. She called them the "Motherline,"[24] the feminine line of descendants, connecting woman to woman and spanning the generations through our stories. Lowinsky recognized that the narrative provided context and application of our lived experiences, connecting grandmothers and great-aunts, mothers and other mothers, those influential and possibly unrelated people in our lives, depositing in us the indelible markings that shape us as individuals and leaders. What is striking is that these narratives are often orally transmitted rather than documented. Like good parables, the stories taught us right from wrong. They nurtured us when we were hurt or harmed. They taught us to care for ourselves and provided a sustaining vision that kept and enabled us. And while we often took for granted that mom was just being mom, our first understanding of leadership may have emerged from Lowinsky's idea of the Motherline because it was the women who most often served as the ones to first shape us.

In addition, however, the narratives collaborate to weave lessons in womanist leadership, which allow us to recognize agency and power. When I declare that my stories are not in the book, I am emboldened to lift narratives that originate from the standpoint of African American women. The experiences that have shaped African American women since arriving to this country in the 1600s are an embedded part of the leadership narrative. If we are to understand leadership from the perspective of the African American woman, then we must understand her standpoint. Additionally, we must value her story. While human nature will seek to compare and favor one perspective over another, it is critical that we promote the African American woman's story, as well as the stories of other marginalized people, as valuable. When I consider my leadership journey and the journeys of other sisters along the way, what stands out is how we have had to navigate marginalization by affirming a self-worth that was societally deprived, engaging in a dogged determination to succeed and demonstrating an unwavering commitment to community in ways that inverted what was meant for harm into that which was for good.

Just as knowledge is expanded through the consideration of multiple standpoints, so the operational leadership framework is expanded when we consider womanist leadership. A womanist leadership approach values the marginalized voices that are typically silenced because it understands the inherent complexities of intersectionality. For example, a leader from the dominant culture can be oblivious to the need for or existence of alternative strategies and tactics for leading because privilege obviates that need and creates unconscious bias. Even when diverse ways of leading are recognized, that strategy might be deemed lesser than. Simply by comparison, preferential attitudes are revealed where masculine ways of leading are inferred as being superior. However, intersectional analysis forces us to engage the potential emergence of multiple standpoints, shaping a complex discourse that cannot be dismissed as an either/or option.

This is what the African American woman's experience reveals: the oppressions of being both black and female. This is, at a minimum, a double bind with which African American women must contend. And this bind has required the development of new patterns and operational models for leadership that deviate from the dominant culture's way of leading because that way of leading was suboptimal given the oppressive systems that overtly and covertly operate in our culture. However, simultaneously, African American women have had to learn and understand the leadership norms of the dominant culture, because this knowledge was necessary to navigate social systems. Again, this expands the leadership framework. Through these multiple lenses from which leadership is viewed and functions, African American women have gained the benefit of an enlarged perspective and an adaptive capacity required to maneuver across multiple systems and contexts. Those who operate in the privilege of the dominant cultural leadership narrative have not needed to develop this capacity because they can take for granted their ways of leading without having to concern themselves with the practices of others. However, by understanding these leadership perspectives derived from alternative standpoints, there is an expanded epistemology that benefits all.

Moreover, this consideration of African American women in leadership expands the framework because it challenges authoritative discourses and reconstructs dominant meanings. According to relational dialectic theory, "social life is a dynamic knot of contradictions, a ceaseless interplay between contrary or opposing tendencies."[25] Through interaction, an institutionalized authoritative tendency or discourse emerges that is recognized as the dominant theory or meaning, whose use is taken for granted. Viewed in this way, the leadership theory that drives pedagogy and operational processes is derived from this male-dominated, Eurocentric, economically advantaged perspective. This is the dominant, authoritative discourse.

We can challenge this perspective, but it cannot be removed because it is so embedded in how we operate. Nevertheless, by challenging the authoritative discourses, multilevel processes emerge that demonstrate incompatibilities.

For example, women recognizing that they could not successfully and sustainably lead in the same ways as men instituted new ways of leading that addressed what was recognized as institutional shortcomings. Their emergent leadership styles were initially regarded as exceptional, in that their styles were considered caveats to the operational norm, rather than indicative of a need-based organizational change. However, "the ongoing experience of contradictory reality [reshaped] the consciousness of institutional inhabitants, and they, in some circumstances, [acted] to fundamentally transform the present social arrangements and themselves."[26] In other words, as more women assumed leadership roles, they helped to redefine the organizations and institutions of which they were a part, changing the view of leadership and their organizations. This work of agency on the part of the emerging organizational leaders drove institutional inhabitants to demand new social interactions.

And this is the type of dynamic change womanist leadership initiates because it is grounded in the dialectic perspective. The dominant, authoritative discourse marginalizes and oppresses those who are not in the majority, but the "social theories emerging from and/or on behalf of U.S. Black women and other historically oppressed groups aim to find ways to escape from, survive in, and/or oppose prevailing social and economic injustice."[27] These social theories serve as the contradictions that drive change and force social interactions to grow. Moreover, the dialectic perspective of womanist leadership is based on the fluid relationship of opposing concepts and founded on the dialectic of oppression and activism. So, although African American women have been systematically oppressed, they have emerged as leaders who are activists. It was bell hooks who noted that, because "we could be affirmed in our minds and hearts despite poverty, hardship, and deprivation,"[28] a safe space was created that made it possible for African American women to demand their rights and "the dignity denied us on the outside in the public world."[28]

This brings me back to my grandmother, Edith Jackson. An authoritative discourse emboldened a 1950s store manager to display a racist depiction contrasting a black washerwoman with a white modern-day homemaker. But my grandmother, affirmed in her mind of a right and just depiction, advocated to the point of civil disobedience, refusing to back down and demanding restoration. Her way of leading, which is a study in dialectic relational theory, expands the leadership framework because it asserts a way of leading that is inclusive of tactics that transcend the dominant structures and practices. It ushers in new ways of leading because it provides space for new voices. The leadership lessons are learned as we glean them from the narratives. In addition, when our gleanings emerge from matrilineal narratives, they truly have the power to transform because these are stories that are most often not in the book.

Lessons in Womanist Leadership

■ Learn leadership through the Motherline. By gleaning from and reflecting upon the story of one's matrilineal ancestry, we can discover lessons of leadership. The matrilineal narrative is particularly powerful because these are the stories that are often discounted when we consider the characteristics of leadership.

■ Lead as your authentic self. We can feel empowered to recognize and celebrate the leadership traits that are unique to our culture without feeling the stress of trying to embody traits that conflict with our identities.

■ Claim your standpoint narrative. Discovering our narrative from our standpoint helps to expand the dialectic perspective and sets the stage for deconstructing marginalizing practices that are drawn from dominant cultural structures.

■ Be a womanist leader. The concept of womanism—an expansive, inclusive, justice-advocating, communally focused way of being that is attributed to African American women—has the power to recast how we view leadership because it encourages an expansive, inclusive, justice-advocating, communally focused way of leading.

Notes

1. A portion of this story was first published by Debora Jackson, "How My Grandmother's Story Helped Me Lead as an African-American Woman," *Faith and Leadership*, July 12, 2016, https://www.faithandleadership.com/debora-jackson -how-my-grandmothers-story-helped-me-lead-african-american-woman, accessed July 26, 2018.

2. Joseph C. Rost, *Leadership for the Twenty-first Century* (New York: Praeger, 1991), 94.

3. Patricia S. Parker, *Race, Gender, and Leadership: Re-Envisioning Organizational Leadership from the Perspectives of African American Women Executives* (2005; New York: Psychology Press, 2015), 9.

4. Sally Helgensen, *The Female Advantage: Women's Ways of Leadership* (New York: Doubleday, 1990), 38.

5. Parker, 9.

6. Ibid.

7. Judy A. Alston and Patrice A. McClellan, *Herstories: Leading with the Lessons of the Lives of Black Women Activists*, Black Studies and Critical Thinking (New York: Peter Lang, 2011), 18.

8. Sandra Harding, ed., *The Feminist Standpoint Theory Reader: Intellectual and Political Controversies* (New York: Routledge, 2004), 5.

9. Amanda K. Sesko and Monica Biernat, "Prototypes of Race and Gender: The Invisibility of Black Women," *Journal of Experimental Social Psychology* 46 (2010), 357.

10. Ibid., 358.

11. Ibid., 360.

12. Courtney Lyons, "Breaking Through the Extra-Thick Stained-Glass Ceiling: African American Baptist Women in Ministry," *Review and Expositor* 110, no. 1 (Winter 2013): 77–91, 82.

13. Patricia Hill Collins, "Learning from the Outsider Within," in *The Feminist Standpoint Theory Reader: Intellectual and Political Controversies*, ed. Sandra Harding (New York: Routledge, 2004), 108.

14. Ibid., 106–7.

15. Marilyn Byrd, "Theorizing African American Women's Leadership Experiences: Socio-Cultural Theoretical Alternatives," *Advancing Women in Leadership* 29, no. 2 (2009), 3.

16. Collins, 110–11.

17. Ibid., 112.

18. Darlene Clark Hine and Kathleen Thompson, *A Shining Thread of Hope: The History of Black Women in America* (New York: Broadway Books, 1998), 308.

19. Harding, 3.

20. Alice Walker, *In Search of Our Mothers' Gardens: Womanist Prose* (New York: Open Road, 1983), xi–xii.

WOMANIST **1.** From *womanish*. (Opp. of "girlish," i.e., frivolous, irresponsible, not serious.) A black feminist or feminist of color. From the black folk expression of mothers to female children, "You acting womanish," i.e., like a woman. Usually referring to outrageous, audacious, courageous or *willful* behavior. Wanting to know more and in greater depth than is considered "good" for one. Interested in grown-up doings. Acting grown up. Being grown up. Interchangeable with another black folk expression: "You trying to be grown." Responsible. In charge. *Serious.* **2.** *Also:* A woman who loves other women, sexually and/or nonsexually. Appreciates and prefers women's culture, women's emotional flexibility (values tears as natural counterbalance of laughter), and women's strength. Sometimes loves individual men, sexually and/or nonsexually. Committed to survival and wholeness of entire people, male *and* female. Not a separatist, except periodically, for health. Traditionally a universalist, as in: "Mama, why are we brown, pink, and yellow, and our cousins are white, beige, and black?" Ans.: "Well, you know the colored race is just like a flower garden, with every color flower represented." Traditionally capable, as in: "Mama, I'm walking to Canada and I'm taking you and a bunch of other slaves with me." Reply: "It wouldn't be the first time." **3.** Loves music. Loves dance. Loves the moon. *Loves* the Spirit. Loves love and food and roundness. Loves struggle. *Loves* the Folk. Loves herself. *Regardless.* **4.** Womanist is to feminist as purple is to lavender.

21. Ibid.

22. Fatema Hayat, "What Is a Womanist," Progressive Pupil, March 4, 2014, https://progressivepupil.wordpress.com/2014/03/04/what-is-a-womanist/, accessed November 6, 2018.

23. Scholar and researcher Clenora Hudson-Weems has sought to more concretely reclaim, name, and define a paradigm specific to the experiences and characteristics of African diasporic women. She coined the term *Africana Womanism*, identifying the Africana woman with 18 qualities, including Self-Namer, Self-Definer, Family-Centered, Genuine in Sisterhood, Strong, In Concert with Male in the Liberation Struggle, Whole, Authentic, Respectful of Elders, Adaptable, Ambitious, and Nurturing. See Clenora Hudson-Weems, *Africana Womanism*, Reclaiming Ourselves (New York: Routledge, 2020).

24. Toni C. King and S. Alease Ferguson, eds., *Black Womanist Leadership: Tracing the Motherline* (Albany: State University of New York Press, 2010), 1.

25. Marnel Niles Goins, "Playing with Dialectics: Black Female Friendship Groups as a Homeplace," *Communications Studies* 62, no. 5 (November–December 2011): 531–46, 533.

26. Myeong-Gu Seo and W. E. Douglas Creed, "Institutional Contradictions, Praxis, and Institutional Change: A Dialectical Perspective," *Academy of Management Review* 27, no. 2 (April 2002): 222–47, 225.

27. Goins, 534.

28. bell hooks, *Yearning: Race, Gender, and Cultural Politics* (Boston: South End Press, 1990), 42.

29. Ibid.

CHAPTER 2

Use What Your Momma Gave You

> Little Sally Walker,
> Sittin' in a saucer
> Ride, Sally, ride
> Wipe your weepin' eyes
> Put your hands on your hips
> And let your backbone slip
> Shake it to the east
> Shake it to the west
> Shake it to the very one
> That you love the best

I remember singing this rhyme as a little girl playing in the neighborhood. For endless hours, my friends and I took turns being Little Sally Walker, using our hip-shaking abilities to identify who would next be "it." And in our play, we would note the one who could really put her hands on her hips and make her backbone slip. It was a badge of honor to be able to undulate, swing, and sway. After all, that's what your momma gave you: hips, a backside, and the capabilities that come with a slipping backbone. But we were not truly aware of ourselves or what we were doing at that age. We were just girls playing. By the time I reached adulthood, I had attributed our play to colloquialism—something unique to northern Indiana. I had no idea that Little Sally Walker's tale was sung in urban neighborhoods across the country. Generations of African American girls learned to put their hands on their hips to let their backbones slip. But again, it did not seem striking until I had the opportunity to travel to Haiti in 2011.

A team of missionaries, organized by the First Baptist Church in Needham, Massachusetts, traveled to Haiti after the devastating 2011 earthquake. We were housed in a retreat center for missionaries in Thomassin, which was home to an orphanage. After spending our days working at a school in Port au Prince, we would return to the retreat center to spend time with the children. I played with girls who ranged in ages from eight to twelve. My Creole was poor, and they spoke no English, other than to ask me if I was there to adopt, a heartbreaking question. However, our play transcended language, and we engaged in the same type of sing-song games that I played as a child. When they led games in Creole, I sang along substituting "da-da-da-da" for the words since I could not speak the language. They did the same if I led the games in English. Imagine my surprise, however, when they started singing the tune of Little Sally Walker. The unmistakable motions of "hands on your hips and let your backbone slip" were telltale. Who knew that even in Haiti, little girls sang about Little Sally Walker?

It was a thrilling moment in which the world became very small. But the moment was emboldening. As these young girls engaged in freeing play, I came to appreciate a cultural awareness that is embedded in women of the African diaspora. When we see ourselves, we see what our mommas gave to us. We see the spherical hair shaft that gives our hair that coarse, even kinky, appearance. We see full nostrils and lips. We recognize a denser bone structure—being big boned, as the old folks would say. As a result, our hips tend to be wider, our buttocks, thighs, and legs fuller. We were differently shaped than women of other cultures, and as our childhood play affirmed, it was wonderful. Maya Angelou put it plainly when she declared we are not "built to suit a fashion model's size."[1] And it did not matter because we were phenomenal nonetheless. Yet, some of these assertions would be challenged in a culture where African Americans were not dominant. I learned this fact first-hand.

I had the opportunity to model for a fashion show in Boston years ago. I was excited about my fitting on Newbury Street, the trendy fashion avenue in Boston. But the fashion show coordinator was less so when she met me. Her distaste was evident as her eyes traveled the length of my body. Finally, in response, she twisted her mouth and said, "I don't know about those hips." You would have thought she had been told to dress an elephant. I am a size 6, for the record. But clearly, the endowment of hindquarters that are attributable to my ancestry were not welcomed by the coordinator who had to provide my wardrobe for the show. I was only trying to use what my momma gave me, but I was made to feel badly about my body image.

This is the heart of the issue for African American women. What our mothers gave us has not been seen historically as positive or of value because black women's bodies have been systematically devalued and declared as grotesque and hated. When Europeans explored the African continent and encountered African people, they immediately made comparisons between themselves and Africans, declaring their culture and standards as superior and normative versus Africans, who were deemed inferior and bestial. But it was the differences in body types that would be the most condemning according to the Europeans who would explore the African continent. The difference in Africans: practices, culture, and bodies were, in their estimation, indicative of something unacceptably negative. "To varying degrees, observers from England, France, Germany, Belgium, and other colonial powers perceived African sensuality, eroticism, spirituality, and/or sexuality as deviant, out of control, sinful, and an essential feature of racial difference."[2] Specific to body type, the rounded buttocks and muscular thighs and legs were seen by Europeans as abnormally animalistic, which led to a prejudicial characterization of Africans as sexualized. The concluding opinion was that black bodies were grotesque and the deemed ugliness of them was disdainful. Notwithstanding, there was a fascination with African bodies, particularly those of women. There was something arousing in this ironic combination of grotesque hatred and insatiable curiosity with the black female body. This is readily seen in the story of Saartjie Baartman.

Born in 1789 in South Africa, Saartjie was taken away from her homeland in 1810 by Alexander Dunlop, a British military doctor, and Hendrick Ceasars, his South African manservant. They saw the opportunity to exploit Saartjie as a scientific oddity. Although Saartjie exhibited genuine talent by singing, dancing, and playing an instrument, it was her physique that made her memorable. Dunlop capitalized on the enormity of Saartjie's buttocks as a "bona fide physiological anomaly" while also creating the allure that her purportedly enlarged genitalia, a supposed feature attributed to Khoisan women,[3] was reflective of a heightened sexual appetite. Her buttocks were thought to be so abnormally large that people flocked to her appearances just to see her. Within months of her arrival, Saartjie Baartman became London's most popular attraction. She was exploited on stage with the name of the Hottentot Venus and paraded about to entertain a paying public. As part of the act, she was adorned in costumes consisting of nothing more than flesh-colored leotards, beads, and feathers, creating an illusion of nakedness that was meant to signify sexual carnality. People paid extra for the opportunity to touch her.

But what did the term "Hottentot Venus" mean? "Hottentot" was a term coined by Dutch colonialists to describe the Khoisan people's Khoi language. The European explorers who traveled to South Africa were unable to master the Khoisan language, "particularly their complex phonology of implosive consonants, or 'clicks.'"[4] Thus, "Hottentot" was a slur meant to deride the misunderstood sounds of the Khoi language and was based on the inability of Europeans to speak the language. The term effectively defined Saartjie as a black other and foreign. And Venus, as in the Roman goddess of love, desire, sexuality, and prostitution, was an overt reference to sexuality.

The term "Hottentot Venus" fueled stereotypes about the body image of this African woman, offering a promise of erotic, bestial fascination. According to artist renderings of the time, Saartjie was endowed with ample breasts, wide hips, rounded buttocks, and large thighs on an otherwise diminutive frame. Her stature was unexceptional for Khoisan women. However, Saartjie's physique was deemed abnormal in nineteenth-century London, playing into Britain's obsession with buttocks, according to chronicler Rachel Holmes. But the term "Hottentot Venus" also "coupled Eros [meaning sexual love] with notions of ugliness, desire with degradation, license with taboo, transcendent goddess with carnal beast."[5] The result was that an African woman and sexuality became equated with ugliness rather than sexual love and desire. But that curiosity fed a perverse desire for what was considered taboo. The viewing public exhibited a lust for that which was African and yet recognized as aesthetically ugly. This lust was enflamed by the manipulative costuming that served to confirm the fantasies that Europeans held about African sexuality, which were believed to be deviant and barbaric. But the curious patrons who flocked to see Saartjie were not considered to be perverse, even though it would have been reprehensible to express outward desire for an African woman. Instead, the narrative was reoriented to suggest that women of African descent were sexually wanton as evidenced by features such as protruding buttocks.

The story is horrific on its own merit, but the exploitation reinforced prejudiced behavior. Saartjie's difference was an acceptable rationale for discrimination. But more important was the fact that physical difference played such a significant role in that discrimination. Saartjie was prejudged for her bodily image, which became the rationale for continued exploitation long after her death in 1815. Saartjie Baartman's remains were sold to the Museum of Natural History in Paris, where she was dissected and her genitalia cast in wax. Saartjie's skeleton, body cast, brain, and genitalia remained on display sometime between 1822 and 1850 until the 1970s.[6] Her remains were finally interred on August 9, 2002.

This mindset of justifiable discrimination based on difference, rooted in European imperialism that condoned the exploitation of the African continent, had deeply embedded itself in Europe in the early nineteenth century and was quickly spreading abroad. Biased practices persistently shaped how African people were regarded in the New World, establishing themselves with the Europeans who settled there. And while the transatlantic slave trade was abolished in the United States in 1808, the mentality of discriminatory treatment based on difference was well-established and continued during the period of enslavement.

Enslaved people of African ancestry were an exploitable commodity. Male and female bodies were commonly poked and prodded, with their genitalia manipulated with carnal fascination. The horrors for women included sexual assault and rape, even though such abuses were never viewed as such. Enslaved women were property with which the owner could do what he pleased. Exploitation was not only acceptable, but it was a right. More egregious, however, was the fact that abuse was justified by a sexualized stereotype based on women's bodies. The abusers claimed not to rape to feed their own desires; they did so under the guise of satisfying the African woman's desire. The accepted societal stereotype believed that the build of African-descended female bodies suggested a need for sexual engagement, and such engagement was a means of maintaining order. This rationale was analogous to the bodily discrimination that declared Saartjie's protruding buttocks to be evidence of sexual wantonness.

But this stigma of abnormal ugliness and contempt for women of African ancestry most poignantly manifested itself when comparing them with women of European ancestry. White women were idealized as the embodiment of "true womanhood" while black women were the embodiment of fallen womanhood. White women were considered pure, chaste, and in need of tenderness and care. They epitomized all that womanhood was. Such a comparison recalls the words of Sojourner Truth, who, in a purportedly impromptu speech, noted a pervasive male attitude that white women needed to be helped into carriages, lifted over ditches, and enjoy the best places. At issue for Truth was that she was also a woman but had never been offered such assistance or care. Her contrasts revealed the societal double standard between white and black women, codifying the vaunted status of white womanhood and the negative status of African American women as fallen or marred. Many of these images were instantiated during the time of enslavement, but once developed and applied, they persisted with lasting indelibility.

The most pervasive image of African American women from slavery is that of Mammy. She is described as

> black in color as well as race and fat with enormous breasts that are full enough to nourish all the children in the world; her head is perpetually covered with her trademark kerchief to hide the kinky hair that marks her as ugly. Tied to her physical characteristics are her personality traits: she is strong, for she certainly has enough girth, but this strength is used in the service to her white master and as a way of keeping her male counterparts in check; she is kind and loyal, for she is a mother; she is sexless.[7]

Again, this is an image of the negative body type of African American women. Mammy was an overweight woman whose ample breasts were given to nurse the children of her owner. Mammy was the symbol of the ideal slave: in charge of all domestic management and deeply loyal to her master. But in contrast with the lady of the house, Mammy was undesirable as a sexual being. Her masculine strength, obesity, and plain physicality served as a foil to the image of a white woman's ultra-femininity. As a result, she was non-threatening. Her physical features, most notably that she was fat and dark-skinned, with enormous breasts and kinky hair, made her ugly.

Where Mammy was sexless, Jezebel thus emerged to represent the overly sexualized African American woman. The roots of this stereotype date back to the sixteenth and seventeenth centuries and result from the allure of the "Negress."[8] This allure, as was seen with Saartjie, created the conditions for violation and dehumanization. Enslaved women were forced to disrobe and subjected to humiliating inspections. Beyond the connotation that they needed sexual engagement, these women were branded as sexually promiscuous and immoral, which further justified the abuses that occurred at the hand of slave-holders, overseers, sons, or other slaves. "The myth that it was impossible to rape Black women because they were already promiscuous helped mask the sexual exploitation of enslaved Black women by their owners."[9] And when black women gave birth to mixed-raced children, white women blamed the enslaved woman for the birth of the child rather than the slaveholding man. This label of Jezebel overall blamed the victim for being regarded as sexualized.

The Matriarch was the strong, masculinized workhorse of a woman. In contrast to the frail, domestic femininity of white women, she was capable of hard labor and physical exertion. Such characterizations have parallels to Saartjie who, like a workhorse, was required to perform endlessly. The fact that she died five years after her premiere at the age of twenty-six suggests that she was worked to death. The Matriarch was also labeled for being domineering. Some women who were stripped of husbands and children due to enslavement became overbearing and even emasculating as they were left to assume traditional male roles.

The emasculating characteristic was applied to Sapphire, the domineering and aggressive woman from the "Amos & Andy" radio show, which first aired in 1928. In contrast to the seeming submissive support given to their partners by white women, Sapphire was known for demeaning and belittling flawed black male characters. Again, we see parallels of Sapphire in Saartjie. During one performance while Saartjie played her guitar, a gentleman patron laughed at her. In anger, she struck him with her musical instrument. Her handlers, wanting to capitalize on the drama, declared Saartjie as being "wild as a beast,"[10] as African savages were thought to be wild.

The Many Ways of Marginalization

These persistent stereotypes that pertain to identity collaborate to weaken the credibility and authority of African American women; however, they also challenge an African American woman's perceived capacity to lead, because they undermine the perceptions of effectiveness.

For example, the "Pine Sol Lady," the African American woman depicted in Pine Sol commercials, is symbolic of Mammy. A contemporary hairstyle notwithstanding, she happily totes bottles of Pine Sol, declaring the house as clean, which is a diminishing characterization because it connects her to servile roles rather than that of leadership. Mammy would not be recognized as a leader and in control because she is supposed to be submissive and happily loyal.

Misogynistic videos commonly portray Jezebel. As scantily clad women are paraded in the media, they continue to feed a sexualized fantasy about black women and reduce them to objects. According to objectification theory, women adopt and internalize an observer's perspective on their physical selves.[11] Thus, their value becomes linked to being viewed as sexually desirable. Moreover, Jezebel would suffer from a sexualized stigma as observers relate her upward progression to bodily endowments rather than merit.

The domineering matriarch is seen in every Tyler Perry *Madea* movie, reinforcing the image of African American women as bossy and domineering. But as the Madea character demonstrates, popular culture has conflated what had been two distinct caricatures of African American women into one. Not only is she seen as domineering, but also she is angry, like Sapphire, which is a particularly condemning moniker. To be labeled angry, according to Michelle Obama, is "another damaging cliché, one that's been forever used to sweep minority women to the perimeter of every room, an unconscious signal not to listen to what we've got to say."[12] It is a way of discrediting a leader and one that I have experienced, being told by a supervisor that I was too aggressive. Given the valued command-and-control style of leadership in men, aggressiveness and assertiveness are viewed positively as male leadership traits; however, these styles are less readily accepted in women. When women attempt to assert themselves in leadership, they are criticized for being aggressive. And when African American women assert themselves, they are criticized for being angry.

Additionally, from the perspective of physical appearance and bodily image, conscious and unconscious bias continues to privilege

European standards of beauty over African standards. As a result, many black people have been convinced that their bodies are, in fact, ugly, primarily because of their color, but also because of their size and shape.[13] Designers like Gloria Vanderbilt and Tommy Hilfiger openly declared that they did not make their clothing to fit black bodies. Hearing the messages, directly or indirectly, African American women and girls cannot help but be affected. If acceptance is predicated to a norm and standard that most will never be able to achieve, consider the impact on one's sense of self-worth. As one fourteen-year-old African American female noted, "Black girls can't be looked at any worse in society than they already are—black and female is pretty high on the list of things not to be." When the self is diminished, the ability to rise above and seek opportunities to lead is hindered.

Stereotypes and Discrimination

These issues are further complicated as the stereotypes associated with gender, race, and identity are conflated. African American women recognize discrimination, but the root reasons are more difficult to discern. Is discrimination the result of gender, racial, or combined gender and racial bias? Or is the discrimination the result of identity bias that ensues from any of these combined categories? When such complexity in the potential for bias is recognized, it is not hard to understand that African American women suffer marginalization in many ways.

Gender and racial bias contributes to the fact that fewer opportunities exist for women and African Americans in leadership. And even when there are opportunities, inequities present themselves. For example, white women earn, on average, 83 cents for every dollar that a white male earns, but African American women earn, on average, 65 cents for every dollar that a white male earns in industry.[14] When I was named chief information officer (CIO) of a company for which I worked, I was compensated at a rate that was 25 percent less than my peers, but I had no idea. My experience was an example of hitting the concrete ceiling, that additional rung in the ladder representing the specific challenges of African American women in the work-place.[15] It is indicative of the unknowable. Whereas a glass ceiling suggests that you can see through to the other side that which is unobtainable for you, a concrete ceiling suggests that you do not know that there is another side to which you can aspire. Such a ceiling affects African American women as they seek executive-level positions. Because there are fewer African Americans and women at these senior levels, aspirants have fewer mentors to provide guidance and help them navigate to the other side of the concrete barrier. It would have never occurred to me that I would be compensated at a lower rate than my C-level peers, but that is the nature of the obstacle. You do not know what you do not know. And in the not knowing, my ignorance was exploited.

To navigate the challenges, realizing acceptance and recognition, some African American women have capitulated, opting to assume the distorted characterizations that serve to marginalize. As Melissa Harris-Perry notes regarding African American women:

> It may be surprising that some gyrate half-naked in degrading hip-hop videos that reinforce the image of black women's lewdness. It may be shocking that some black women actors seem willing to embody the historically degrading image of Mammy by accepting movie roles where they are cast as the nurturing caretakers of white women and children. It may seem inexplicable that a respected black woman educator would stamp her foot, jab her finger in a black man's face, and scream while trying to make a point on national television, thereby reconfirming the notion that black women are irrationally angry.[16]

The desire to gain acceptance or realize recognition is paid at the expense of selfhood by reinforcing stereotypes. Harris-Perry notes that she was the "respected black woman educator" screaming on television. Challenging what she viewed as an erroneous assertion made by another commentator, Harris-Perry found herself in a shouting match. Her intent was to defend her point, but the result was less than flattering. People did not remember the strength of her argument; they remembered what confirmed the stereotype of the angry black woman.

Another means of acceptance is realized through racial ambiguity. What is deemed as beautiful in our culture is based on a European standard, and those who conform most closely to that standard are recognized as beautiful. History shows that some people of African ancestry whose European ancestry is dominant have been able pass, which means to be mistaken as white, where Jim Crow–era laws dictated that an individual who had any African ancestry, even one drop, be classified as black or Negro.

These same people can declare themselves as multiracial today. This is marvelously progressive, but it presents a different challenge for African American women and what is conceptualized as beautiful. Increasingly there is a trend to identify beautiful women of color as multiracial rather than recognizing them as black or African American. For example, women such as Oscar-winning actress Hallie Berry, pop star and model Zendaya, or Meghan Markle, the Duchess of Sussex, have one African American parent and one white parent. Today these women are commonly recognized as multiracial, which seems to make it acceptable to declare them beautiful. It implicitly reinforces a message that to be black or African American is contrary to beauty. Black is not beautiful. And if these women are recognized as beautiful, then they cannot be declared as black. The message seems clear: beauty for African American women is rooted in ambiguous skin color, straight hair, and "European" features.

African American women have attempted to conform to such imposed standards of beauty to be accepted or to progress in their careers, and hair represents a significant area of conformity. According to a study that examined body type image concerns for African American college-aged women,[17] participants who worked in predominantly white workspaces reported feeling the necessity to wear their hair in relaxed or permed styles rather than natural to be accepted. Chemical-based products were most commonly used to achieve straight, smooth hairstyles. As one women noted, "Hair determines, in mainstream America, where or how far you get."[18] Women who wore their hair naturally feared being labeled as radical, which could result in loss of financial or career opportunities.[19] A former colleague's experience is related to this point. She spoke of an employer who offered to buy her a wig to cover her short-cropped, natural hairstyle, which he saw as unattractive. When she refused a wig, the employer asked her if she could grow her hair.

Skin tone is another challenging aspect of body image for African Americans. Women noted that darker-skinned African American women were viewed as less attractive, less likely to achieve, and not suitable romantic partners compared with lighter-skinned African American women.[20] I have heard dark-skinned women express feelings of rejection because of their color. These perceptions of diminished self-worth can be important predictors of academic success and income potential.[21] Additionally, the perceptions of discrimination based on color have long-term impacts because they can influence African American women's sense of body image satisfaction. In response, women in some African diasporic countries practice skin bleaching to achieve a lighter complexion, using damaging chemicals without concern for the effect. "There is the widespread perception in this context that in order to achieve the status that goes along with being brown or socially white, one has to alter the way one wears their skin and the complexion that they project."[22]

Use What Your Momma Gave You

Given these many challenging obstacles that are related to body image and the marginalizing discrimination that results, how then are African American women to use what our mommas gave us in favorable ways? African American girls who may have gloried in their bodies while playing Little Sally Walker find themselves in a society where they are consciously and unconsciously told that they are ugly and inferior. Moreover, these images, coupled with additional forms of discrimination, create obstacles that make it more difficult for African American women to prosper in general, let alone ascend to leadership positions. As a result, it would be no surprise to see Little Sally Walker sitting in a saucer and weeping. But just as the rhyme encourages Sally to rise and dry her weeping eyes, so African American women must rise above the stereotypes to reclaim the glory of our bodies. In other words, "put your hands on your hips and let your backbone slip." Not everyone can do this. Unless you are adequately endowed, not much will happen when you attempt such slippage. And just like we used to celebrate the girl who could "work it," we need to reclaim that spirit of celebration of our bodies as adult women. That reclamation will strengthen our witness and prepare us to lead.

How do we do this? We first must remember that we are made in the image of God. Genesis 1:27 tells us that "God created humankind in [God's] image," in God's nature, "God created male and female." All human beings were created with God's essence—that life-giving dynamism that animates and moves us. We were all endowed with gifts and abilities to know, discern, and exercise awareness. With these abilities, we are called to recognize that there is no hierarchy in humanity. We are all created equal in the sight of God. Unfortunately, humanity has too commonly used its God-given abilities of knowledge and discernment to discriminate against those who are different. For example, there is no such classification as a white race, but society adopted a standard that associated skin color and ethnicity to attribute positive characteristics to people of a certain ancestry over others. To be white connotes rightness and light, which further suggests superiority. To be black suggests darkness or evil. These connotations have been attached to people as a means of marginalization. But these categorizations are false demarcations. Genetics demonstrates that skin color differences do not translate to biological differences. We are made in the image of God, which means that each of us has that divine spark that is the essence of God.

But perhaps the more important idea that justifies reclaiming the celebratory spirit of our bodies can be found in Genesis 1:31: God looked over everything God made and saw that it was good; so very good. God saw God's creation as imbued with value, worth, and importance. This is significant for African American women because images in media or societal preferences suggest otherwise. Given a steady barrage, such negative images become internalized to an extent that they exist as unchallenged and ultimately accepted as factual. To declare, however, our inherent goodness begins to counteract the narrative. It is reminiscent of the Shulamite woman in the Song of Solomon. She says, "I am black, but comely."[23] Instead of accepting the negative stigma of blackness, she declares that she is beautiful regardless. She asserts her worth. In fact, her beauty, desirability, and worth were accentuated in this love poem. And these assertions were affirmed by a partner who loved her. It was not a leap to suggest that the woman was effectively saying "I am good," which was correlated to creation. Having been made in God's image, we as created beings are good.

This sets the stage to claim, or reclaim if need be, a sense of self-worth. My faith tells me that I have worth because my body is a temple in which God's Spirit dwells, as the apostle writes in 1 Corinthians 6:19. It is a faith that says that if God would dwell here, then I am not beyond redemption or hope. In my redeemable state, I am somebody. It is not just me; this is a collective epistemology. We are somebodies, and this knowledge is a source of empowerment. People of privilege may not need this type of affirmation because every implicit and explicit societal message confirms their worth. However, when people are stripped of personhood through the same implicit and explicit messages that favor some over others, a means to reclaim self-worth is necessary. The reclamation allows us to recognize an authentic sense of self that is not predicated on the definitions of others. With a recovered sense of self, people are emboldened to lead because they realize a self-efficacy that affirms their ability to succeed.

In the face of such contentions, African American women must tap into the same pride of culture and our bodies that they learned to exhibit as children. With hands on hips, they must reclaim worth and beauty. There is a need for declarations that say:

> I came out of a tradition where those things are valued; where you talk about a woman with big legs and big hips and black skin. I came out of a black community where it was all right to have heavy hips and to be heavy. You didn't feel that people didn't like you. The values that infer you must be skinny come from another culture. Those are not the values that I was given by the women who served as my models. I refuse to be judged by the values of another culture. I am a black woman and I will stand as best I can in that imagery.[24]

This is what must be asserted as African American women. Celebrate "thickness" and brown skin. To have "some meat on the bones" was a positive status and certainly more characteristic of women of the African diaspora. As these truths are asserted collectively, women will achieve a greater sense of self-worth.

I would also note that African American women of all sizes and shapes should take pride in the fact that they have learned to invert negative stereotypes for the good. For each of the body image stereotypes, African American women have masterfully subverted the negative for positive ends. For example, Mammy, in her non-threatening and innocuous state, quietly ran the show. As an entity unseen by the slaveholder, Mammy used her persona to get things done. The matriarch and Sapphire may have been viewed as domineering, but compensating for the demasculinization or absence of African American men, their strength became sources of enablement. Even Jezebel could use demureness as a means of getting her way. Stereotypes meant for harm have been critically employed by African American women to influence situations as needed, and because of continued marginalization, African American women have retained the capacity to appropriate adeptly various personas. Whether provocation, dominance, or complicity was used, that ability to reverse in chameleon-like fashion what was meant to negate serves African American women well.

I would additionally assert that African American women can feel emboldened to assert an embodied sense of beauty that is independent of broader societal acceptance. It is interesting that as some of the cultural body images attributed to African ancestry are being appropriated by others, there is greater positive recognition. For example, in 2017, *Sports Illustrated* featured Ashley Graham on the cover of the swimsuit edition. This was a milestone moment because Ashley Graham is not the size 0, thin waif of a model typically featured. She is a size 16, curvy model. Suddenly to be designated as curvy became acceptable. However, African American women can celebrate the fact that they were curvy women before the world became aware of Ashley Graham. Similarly, African American women have been known for having "junk in the trunk," a rounded posterior, before anyone knew of a Kardashian. Rather than rely on the affirmation from changed societal opinions, African American women can assert their self-worth and beauty by remembering their history and what was valued as beautiful. As W. E. B. DuBois said, "I honor the women of my race. Their beauty—their dark and mysterious beauty of midnight eyes, crumpled hair, and soft, full-featured faces . . . No other woman on earth could have emerged from the hell of force and temptation which once engulfed and still surrounds black women in America with half the modesty and womanliness they retain."[25]

African American people must also defend these standards of beauty—not beauty for a black person but as universal beauty. Author Damon Young speaks of this in terms of Michelle Obama. He described Mrs. Obama as a woman blessed with a curvy behind and a beauty specific to blackness that was not a specifically black beauty. He claimed, "She wasn't stunning for a black woman. She was a woman whose undeniable black features made her stunning."[26] On the surface, this may seem like an ironic statement. The challenging proclivity is to compare someone with another and to deem one more favorably than the other. Thus, if comparing Mrs. Obama with what the fashion industry would define as a standard of beauty, she may not have been deemed as beautiful. But in his essay Young was not making such a comparison. He was recognizing the features of a woman who was unmistakably of African ancestry and noting her in her entirety as stunning. And there was an overwhelming pride in this fact. She was beautiful, and because she was seen as beautiful, African American men and women took exception to demeaning comments about her. African Americans took exception not only because she was the First Lady and deserving of the respect accorded to her position but also because this statuesque, distinctly African American woman redefined beauty and allowed other African American women to claim value and worth based on our cultural body image.

And as African American women exhibit pride in their beauty and defend these standards of beauty, others will as well. In 2008, when Mrs. Obama shared that her outfit worn as a guest on the talk show *The View* was purchased at the national clothing retailer White House/Black Market, the store was overwhelmed by women who clamored to purchase the $148.00 dress.[27] An African American woman was being recognized as fashionably trend-setting. Moreover, designers were designing clothing distinctly for an African American body type, which was culturally affirming. As women used what their mommas gave them, they could live into a greater sense of worth.

Leading as an African American Woman

How then do these realities inform leadership from the perspective of an African American woman? Admittedly, they create a challenging landscape. At the foundation, I would contend that many African American girls share the gleeful experience of sing-song games where hip shaking was a celebrated part of the play. Harkening to Genesis 2:25, where humanity in its newly created state was naked and not ashamed, there was no shame in the knowledge of our body. We could glory in our God- and momma-given attributes.

But innocence cannot last when overt and covert messages threatened to sabotage a positive self-image. This was certainly my experience growing up in predominantly white communities. I felt the sting of difference from hair that was far less than care-free to the embarrassment I felt as white friends spent their summers trying to tan as dark as I was. I also remember the media images that were less than affirming. What was seen in movies, television, or magazines did not represent people who looked like me. And if African Americans were represented, it was in a secondary or subservient capacity. These messages had a way of blunting the psyche and challenging how one comes to view one's worth. When messages assert diminished worth, ugliness, or undesirability, you start to believe it.

These negative stigmas and low self-esteem can have damaging impact as African American women come into adulthood. I have spoken with many women who, particularly in ministry, have noted a reticence in advocating for themselves in terms of salary or role. Doubts of self-worth and fears regarding the appropriateness of asking for more cause many women to remain silent during negotiations. Then, with narrowed options and fewer role models, young women may struggle to find mentors who can help to challenge negative perceptions. This has been true for me both academically and vocationally, as I have often been the first or only African American, woman, or African American woman in various roles. Unfortunately, my story is common when senior leadership opportunities are considered. There are no African American women CEOs of Fortune 500 companies, and African American women make up less than 2 percent of middle managers.[28] The statistics for church leadership are similarly stark. According to a 2015 *Christianity Today* article, women represent 10 percent of all Protestant senior pastors,[29] but this is inclusive of all women. While there are African American women senior pastors, the numbers are negligible. Thus, African American women constantly have to blaze trails where the paths are unchartered and difficult with fewer support systems.

In response, paths of least or lesser resistance become attractive. But unfortunately, those paths are often ones pocked with stereotypes. African American women are more readily welcomed into supporting roles rather than senior leadership roles. With parallels to dutiful Mammy, entry-level or lower-level management positions are filled with African American women in the corporate workplace. As line management, African American women are relied upon to support operations. The same phenomenon is seen in the black church, where African American women are welcomed predominantly as pulpit associates in supporting roles.

African American women are also well-received in roles that feed the sexualized stereotype. For example, Josephine Baker was a Paris sensation in the 1920s in performances that accentuated and featured her behind. She capitalized on the white eroticization of black bodies by expressively calling attention to her behind during her dance routines. Tina Turner, a fantasy creation of her then-husband, Ike Turner, with a name given to recall the wild women of early television series, wowed audiences with energetic and sexually stimulating, gyrating performances. Today, artists like Beyoncé and Nicki Minaj, whose rump-shaking abilities rival any, are internationally celebrated. But are their images only perpetuating the stereotypes that have dogged women of African descent for centuries? Are they functioning as modern-day Negresses, Hottentot Venuses, or Jezebels, whose body images serve only to reinforce the stigma that African American women are sexual deviants demonstrating an inherent carnality? I cheer their success but cannot help but voice concern.

As an African American woman who wants to use what my momma gave me, I see the opportunity to build upon a foundation of celebration, mitigate the negative images that demean body types, and steer away from conforming stereotypes that contribute to marginalization. This opportunity can be realized through affirmation. As a leader, I am grounded in the knowledge that God loves me. God loves God's creation, having given Jesus Christ for each of us. This perfect love sets the stage for self-love. This means that I can love myself and, as such, love what my momma gave me. This has not always been the case. I have traversed the phases of the chunky girl, shapeless teen, and young adult with flaring hips to finally reach contentment. It does not mean that I have attained a perfect size or image. It means that I have come to appreciate who I am and how I look. Psalm 139:14 affirms that I am fearfully and wonderfully made, and at my stage of life, it matters less now what others think.

This kind of affirmation is important for all people, but particularly for African American women. Authors such as Audre Lorde and bell hooks have noted that black women must love ourselves. We must overcome the forces that have caused self-hatred, and we must think of ourselves in positive and affirming ways. Doing so begins with understanding the forces that have produced hostility toward blackness and femaleness, but it also means learning new ways to think about ourselves. As such, in my proud contentment and self-love, I feel empowered to dress in ways that are flattering for me, including when I don my clerical robes. I am small in size and stature, and as such, I cannot buy clergy attire off the rack because it is too big. But more than that, I do not want a man's robe cut down to size for a woman. I do not want boxy garb that makes me look asexual. I want attire that is made for women—that celebrates and accentuates the curves that women have, including those that are indicative of my culture. I am not shapeless, and I refuse to dress as though I were.

And in loving myself, I can exude a confidence that expresses my comfort. Short of conceit, it is a sense of certainty that is unapologetic and sure. Because I am aware of my body, I can use it in ways that help me lead. For example, in my consulting work, consultants were coached to use their bodies to crowd the space of clients to encourage participation. Invading space discomforts, and it becomes a psychological strategy to motivate people who are reticent to participate. Many of my colleagues were less comfortable with this tactic because it provoked anxiety for the consultant as well. But because I was comfortable in my skin, it was always a preferred strategy. Similarly, I am emotive with my body as I work with others. During counseling, I might lean in or, if appropriate, touch a hand or the arm of a counselee. As a speaker, I move as I present, often stepping away from a podium or lectern and offering a stance that is open and welcoming. These strategies are meant to attract and to draw people closer in the moment. But they work only when one is comfortable with their body and with themselves. As a leader who is an African American woman, coming to that place of comfort has been significant.

However, attaining this actualized sense of self does not mean that it has come without challenges. As a college student, I had the experience of being sexually harassed by a teaching assistant. I went to him for help but instead spent time evading unwanted touches as he chased me around an office. His excuse was that I was exotic looking. Early in my career, I dealt with the unwanted advances of a coworker who thought it acceptable to attempt throwing candies down my blouse. When I reported him, I was told that perhaps if I did not dress as I did I would not have such issues. Even in pastoral ministry, I have dealt with sexual innuendo and advances. I have had male congregants who thought it appropriate to make provocative comments about my body or my attire. My bodily self-confidence does not mean that advances or incendiary comments are welcomed or desired, and it has felt unfair to be plagued by such blatant abuses.

Thus, I have come to appreciate that my bodily self-confidence has given me voice. As a sexually harassed college student, I did not report my aggressor because I feared that I would not be believed. A few years later, as a relatively new employee who was warding off advances, I reported my colleague. My report was trivialized, but I made the report and refused to accept imposed criticism. These experiences emboldened me as a pastor. Feeling confident in my bodily image and attire, when off-color comments were made, I confronted the offensive statements. I learned that I could forcefully rebuff a remark, offer correction, and remain pastoral. It has been important in my leadership to navigate such a challenge. People do need to know when their words are inappropriate, particularly where someone's body is concerned. But they need to hear those words of rebuke in love so that they can learn from the lesson and make different choices for the future. This is true in advocating for self, but it is also true in advocating for others. Leaders need to be outspoken when others are being shamed or maligned for their looks, appearance, or because of perceived difference. We are all children of God and made in the image of God. Because God has declared each created being as good, how can we do any less?

This awareness of self enables me to encourage self-confidence in and be an advocate for others. If someone is well-dressed and smartly coiffed, I let them know. Few of us can meet the standards that society might deem beautiful, and as such, we carry the baggage of body images that we wish could change. But when someone notices and acknowledges you and how you look, it is affirming. Therefore, we as leaders need to do our part to create a culture that encourages affirmation. I find that this is particularly important for marginalized people, because too often we are socialized to believe that there is room for only one of us. We have gravitated to this belief that a team can have only a finite number of women or minorities; thus, we become territorial as a woman or minority if we feel our place is being threatened. Once threatened, we tear the other down rather than affirm. But being comfortable in myself, I can affirm others who are beautiful or well-dressed without feeling like such compliments detract from me. In other words, if a woman has it going on, I say so, and in doing so, I make alliances and build community.

And when appropriate, I believe that we can help in our capacity as leaders by advising in love when others are not put together in the most flattering ways. Of course, this must be exercised with caution lest we be guilty of imposing a culturally or societally discriminating norm on others. But when appropriate, this kind of mentorship can be empowering. I once had a church administrator who came to the office with a very low-cut blouse such that her breast tattoos were showing. I had no qualm with her tattoos but thought their display at the church was not appropriate. However, rather than sharply criticize, I explained to my assistant that she was a beautiful young woman who did not need to dress so provocatively. I affirmed her while encouraging her to make different choices, especially for the workplace.

Finally, my awareness of self and comfort in my body has increased my awareness of others. I have learned to observe when people are comfortable and when they are not. As a leader, I want to help people feel good about themselves so that they can contribute their gifts and abilities as God intended. Self-awareness and self-love pave the way for such generativity. When we are aware of and love ourselves, we extend that capacity to others, inviting them to do likewise. Through a leadership style that is motivated by bodily self-love, we can help people use what their mommas gave them. Our cultural endowments may be different, but in our embodied flesh, we are encouraged to be our best selves so that we can help others be their best as well. It is this move that transcends stereotypes and allows us to reclaim the joy of a little girl's childhood play—to gleefully put her hands on her hips and let her backbone slip.

Lessons in Womanist Leadership

■ You are good. Being created in the image of God and affirmed as good, we are encouraged to reclaim the joy of our bodily image, exercising self-love even as God loves us.

■ You are loved. We as leaders can encourage in others that love of self and realization of God's love.

■ Be an embodied leader. As we become comfortable with our bodies, we can use our embodied ways of being to enhance our leadership.

■ Use your voice. Having been systematically discriminated against for body image, African American women can be aware of marginalizing stereotypes and be empowered to use their voices to speak against them.

■ Don't hate and perpetuate. Other leaders, understanding stereotypes and stigmas that have been levied against African American women, can operate with greater awareness and not perpetuate stereotypical behavior.

Notes

1. Maya Angelou, *The Complete Collected Poems of Maya Angelou* (New York: Random House, 1994), 130.

2. Patricia Hill Collins, *Black Sexual Politics: African Americans, Gender, and the New Racism* (New York: Routledge, 2004), 98.

3. Rachel Holmes, *African Queen: The Real Life of the Hottentot Venus* (New York: Random House, 2007), 39.

4. Ibid., 9.

5. Ibid., 40.

6. Ibid., 103.

7. Barbara Christian, *Black Women Novelists: The Development of a Tradition, 1892–1976* (Westport, CT: Greenwood Publishing Group, 1980), 11–12.

8. Patricia S. Parker, *Race, Gender, and Leadership: Re-Envisioning Organizational Leadership from the Perspectives of African American Women Executives* (2005; New York: Psychology Press, 2015), 35.

9. Hill Collins, 101.

10. Holmes, 48.

11. Barbara L. Fredrickson and Tomi-Ann Roberts, "Objectification Theory: Toward Understanding Women's Lived Experiences and Mental Health Risks," *Psychology of Women Quarterly* 21 (1997), 177.

12. Michelle Obama, *Becoming* (New York: Crown Publishing, 2018), 265.

13. Farah Jasmine Griffin, "Textual Healing: Claiming Black Women's Bodies, the Erotic Resistance in Contemporary Novels of Slavery," *Callaloo* 19, no. 2 (Spring 1996), Emerging Women Writers: A Special Issue, 521.

14. Elise Gould and Jessica Schieder, "Black and Hispanic Women Are Paid Substantially Less Than White Men," Economic Snapshot, Economic Policy Institute, March 7, 2017, http://www.epi.org/publication/black-and-hispanic-women-are-hit-particularly-hard-by-the-gender-wage-gap/, accessed October 17, 2019.

15. Jacqueline M. Johnson, "The Leadership Styles and Behaviors of African American Women Executives Across Multiple Economic Sectors," *International Journal of Arts & Sciences* (2015): 405–14; see 408.

16. Melissa V. Harris-Perry, *Sister Citizen: Shame, Stereotypes, and Black Women in America* (New Haven, CT: Yale University Press), 29.

17. Germine H. Awad, Carolette Norwood, Desire S. Taylor, Mercedes Martinez, Shannon McClain, Bianca Jones, Andrea Holman, and Collette Chapman-Hilliard, "Beauty and Body Image Concerns Among African American College Women," *Journal of Black Psychology* 41, no. 6 (2015), 554.

18. Ibid.

19. Ibid.

20. Laurel B. Watson, Jioni A. Lewis, and Anahvia Taiyib Moody, "A Social Cultural Examination of Body Image Among Black Women," *Body Image* (2019), https://doi.org/10.1016/j.bodyim.2019.03.008, 4.

21. Ibid.

22. Imani M. Tafari-Ama, "Historical Sociology of Beauty Practices: Internalized Racism, Skin Bleaching, and Hair Straightening," *IDEAZ* 14 (2016), 13.

23. Song of Solomon 1:5, KJV.

24. Dorothy Winbush Riley, ed., *Black Women in the Image of God* (Cleveland, OH: The Pilgrim Press, 1999), 61.

25. Ibid., 60.

26. Damon Young, "Crushing on Michelle," in *The Meaning of Michelle: Sixteen Writers on the Iconic First Lady and How Her Journey Inspires Our Own*, ed. Veronica Chambers (New York: St. Martin's Press, 2017), 41.

27. Mike Celizic, "Michelle Obama Makes $148 Frock a Fashion Smash," *Today*, June 20, 2008, https://www.today.com/news/michelle-obama-makes-148-frock-fashion-smash-wbna25280708, accessed December 21, 2017.

28. Ellen McGirt, "The Black Ceiling: Why African-American Women Aren't Making It to the Top in Corporate America," *Fortune*, September 27, 2017, http://fortune.com/2017/09/27/black-female-ceos-fortune-500-companies/, accessed October 17, 2019.

29. Ashley Emmert, "The State of Female Pastors," *Christianity Today*, October 15, 2015, https://www.christianitytoday.com/women-leaders/2015/october/state-of-female-pastors.html, accessed October 17, 2019.

CHAPTER 3

If It Had Not Been for the Lord on My Side

"If it had not been for the Lord on my side, where would I be? Where would I be?" African Americans take the words of this old hymn to heart, as evidenced by engagement in matters of faith and religion. African Americans far exceed the general population in the United States regarding religious practice, according to a 2014 Pew Religious Landscape Study.[1] Eighty-three percent of African Americans indicate with absolute certainty that God exists, and 82 percent of African Americans describe themselves as belonging to a religious group. Seventy-five percent say that religion is very important in their lives, and 73 percent put that belief in practice by praying at least daily. According to this report, African Americans stand out as the most religiously committed racial or ethnic group in the nation. But as the numbers are analyzed, what we see is the impact of the women. African American women are truly the most religiously observant group in the United States with 83 percent classified as highly religious, meaning that religion is very important to them; they attend religious services at least once a week, pray at least once a day, and believe in God with absolute certainty. African American church membership is estimated to be at least 75 percent female.[2] Truly, African American women dominate the congregation during weekly worship. But in an age where the fastest-growing religious group are those declaring no religious affiliation, what keeps African American women committed to faith? What is it about religious practice that causes African American women to remain so firmly rooted?

These questions are best answered by considering the spirituality of African American people, because their spiritual rootedness can be traced to the spirituality and spiritual permanence of enslaved

Africans who came to the United States. Scholars have refuted the contention of such permanence given that so many were stolen from their homelands at early ages, presumably before faith practices were rooted. And yet despite kidnapping, enslavement, and the brutal Middle Passage, that trade route transporting millions of Africans to the Americas, ways of worship featuring distinctive, African-rooted spiritual practices remained. For example, for the African, worship consisted of singing, shouting, dancing, and using the body as an instrument. People would stomp their feet, clap hands in syncopated rhythms, and create varied musical pitches through voice inflection and an embodied vocalization realized by slapping one's chest, thighs, knees, or legs. Thus, music was a vital component, for in the words of an African dictum, "The spirit will not descend without song."[3] The descending spirit gave utterance to spontaneous prayer and praise. Because these practices were so deeply embedded, Africans in America converted to Christianity gradually, demonstrating a new syncretistic tradition that combined elements of both African and Christian ideas.[4] Christian doctrine had to find expression in these African ways of worship, an effort made difficult because of the antagonistic version of Christianity offered to enslaved peoples.

Howard Thurman recalled that while he had the responsibility of reading the Bible aloud to his grandmother, who was born a slave, she would never allow him to read the Pauline epistles, except for 1 Corinthians 13. Unwilling to question his grandmother in his youth, he said, "with a feeling of great temerity I asked her one day why it was that she would not let me read any of the Pauline letters."[5] She explained that during enslavement, the master's minister would preach to the slaves, and several times a year, the text was drawn from the writings of Paul. Specifically, they were told, "Slaves, be obedient to them that are your masters." The minister would then explain how it was God's will that they were slaves, but that if they were good and obedient, God would bless them.

Given such messages that reinforced enslavement and subjection as a biblical mandate, it would be logical to conclude that the enslaved would reject the religion of slaveholding masters, particularly denouncing a God who willed such a cruel institution. Yet, this was not the case. As Thurman's grandmother asserted, rather than rejecting the faith, she promised her Maker "that if I ever learned to read and if freedom ever came, I would not read that part of the Bible."[6] The Christianity taught to slaves distorted the gospel, asserting that oppression was mandated and their inferiority was God-ordained. But enslaved people developed a hermeneutical perspective that insisted on their full acceptance as people made in the image of God. From the book of Exodus, people of African ancestry saw themselves in the narratives of the Hebrew slaves, with masters being like the hardened-hearted Pharaoh to whom Moses declared, "Let my people go." This assertion is most clearly seen in the Negro spiritual, "Go Down, Moses," which "chronicles the liberating act of God on behalf of the oppressed."[7]

Additionally, people of African ancestry saw themselves in the biblical narratives that spoke affirmatively of Ethiopia, Cush, and Egypt. For instance, the Queen of Sheba, as noted in 1 Kings 10:1-10 and 13, was a black woman. The Shulamite woman in Song of Solomon 1:5 declared, "I am black, and comely." The Bible also chronicles early African civilizations, thus contradicting a white notion of African inferiority. The Canaanites "built great cities across the Jordan and resisted the invading Israelites for centuries."[8] The Ethiopian Pharaoh Tirhakah aided Hezekiah during the Assyrian invasion.[9] Egypt was one of the earliest civilizations whose history was recorded in the Bible. These and other interpretations engendered racial pride and helped African Americans to refute the notion of a Hamitic curse, which suggested that the descendants of Ham, of which peoples of Africa were identified to be, were cursed to forever serve their brothers.[10]

But most notably, African Americans saw in Jesus Christ a Savior who had a penchant for the poor. When Jesus declared he was anointed "to bring good news to the poor, . . . to proclaim release to the captives, . . . to let the oppressed go free,"[11] African Americans recognized in him a personal Savior who was the incarnate God on their side. Jesus understood what it meant to be poor and oppressed, because he was poor and oppressed. He also understood what it meant to be an ethnic other, both from his early childhood in Egypt and in adulthood living in Roman-occupied Palestine. Yet, as the Son of God, Jesus was the messianic hero who would ultimately right the wrongs of this world by making the last first and the first last. Jesus' story was a parallel story to African Americans in the United States, and this reality inspired hope to persevere.

Specifically, African Americans related to Jesus in his rejection and found hope in his triumph. Looking to Isaiah 53, African Americans saw Jesus as the one who was despised by others. He was a man of suffering and acquainted with infirmities because he carried them to the cross. His sacrifice for humanity's sins brought wholeness because by his bruises all are healed. In dying for our sins, Jesus healed the enmity between God and humanity, which emboldened African Americans to recognize themselves as the redeemed of God regardless of what a dominant culture espoused. Moreover, because Jesus overcame death on the cross, through him, African Americans found the power to overcome as well. Therefore, "Jesus liberates us from the crushing burden of otherness and difference, bringing to light the God in us."[12] As a result, African Americans came to claim this Jesus as their own, embracing a Christ-centered way of life that was not only grounded in faith but also motivated them to live that faith out in community through witness and service. To be followers of Christ compelled African American believers to share the soul-saving good news with others so that they too would realize hope in Jesus.

But these rationalized arguments that explain the African American embrace of Christianity are too cerebral to reveal the core of a deeply held belief. For African Americans, the embrace of Christianity was enlivened in the heart and soul and made manifest in part through song, which again harkens back to African spirituality. The theological constructs that have been the source of centuries-long debates by academic scholars are simply and beautifully articulated in the African American spirituals. To say "there is a balm in Gilead" declares that salvation is obtainable through Jesus Christ because he is the balm that heals a sin-sick world. To sing "Jesus is a rock in a weary land" speaks of the power of perseverance in faith. Noting "if it had not been for the Lord on my side, where would I be?" speaks of God's grace through hardship and trial. The songs also asserted God's intent for humanity. When enslaved African Americans sang that they were going to "steal away to Jesus," its dual meaning spoke of faith in Jesus but also the right to be free. Freedom was more boldly asserted through the questioning song refrain "Didn't my Lord deliver Daniel?" If the Lord delivered Daniel, "then why not every man?" And the songs spoke of an eschatological reality promising "soon I will be done with the troubles of the world; I'm going home to live with God."

Thus, African Americans created a belief system inculcated in African expressions of worship and synthesized from biblical texts in the Judeo-Christian story. This belief system left a legacy that continues to vivify the African American church today. The belief practices and worship attendance of African American people are evidence of that lasting cultural inheritance. As the Pew study reports, 79 percent of African Americans regard religion as very important with 15 percent saying that it was somewhat important.[13] Such statistics reveal an embraced belief where African American people came to see themselves as God's people, made in God's image, and the worship experience of the church was a place to celebrate that reality.

African American Women and the Biblical Narrative

Just as African Americans people needed to see themselves in the biblical narrative to claim it as their own, so too African American women have needed to specifically see themselves. Liberation theology emerged as a theological discourse in the 1950s and 1960s, informing the ways that oppressed people are physically freed, spiritually empowered, and culturally affirmed in God. It was the explication of that syncretistic conversion process that enabled African Americans to see themselves rightfully free and included as a people of God through Jesus Christ. In similar suit, womanist theology emerged as a strand of liberation theology. It considered the unique realities of the faith and religious practices of African American women especially focusing on the complex lived experiences that encompassed race, gender, socioeconomic conditions of class and income, and sexuality. "Womanist theology starts with analysis of roles assigned to African American women by their families and the dominant culture, the persistent stereotypes about black women, the combination of race with gender, and recognition of diversity among women."[14] These experiences shape how African American women have made theological meaning in their contexts, constructing the questions where is God and what does it mean to live a life committed to God?

Through whom, then, do African diasporic women see themselves in the biblical narrative? Womanist theologians have lifted Hagar as an exemplar. Hagar was the Egyptian slave girl whom Sarai gave to Abram when she was unable to bear children. Like enslaved African American women, Hagar's consent was not solicited. She was property to be used as the owner desired, and in this case, sexually taken for the purposes of procreation. However, when Hagar conceived, Sarai was angered. Hagar's pregnancy provided the perception of equality, a point of contention for Sarai as matriarch. In response, Sarai rebuked Abram for Hagar's disrespect, which led him to reaffirm his wife's status and authority where an enslaved woman was concerned. Thus emboldened, Sarai beat Hagar, which caused Hagar to run away. When the angel of the Lord found Hagar in the wilderness, he asked, "Where have you come from and where are you going?" Although Hagar shared her intent to escape, the angel told Hagar to return to her mistress and submit to her. He also told her that she would bear a son, whom she would name Ishmael because God had heard her cry. And Hagar praised the God who sees, for God had seen her plight and given heed to her affliction. In short, the Lord was on her side.

Hagar's story is that of the enslaved African American woman. Like Hagar, African American women were subject to sexual abuse and rape. They were exploited by slave owners, overseers, and even other slaves for the purposes of bearing children to extend the workforce. Children born of the forced arrangements between the slave owner and the enslaved heightened the conflict with the slave-owning mistresses who resented the "mulatto" progeny. Given these parallels, African American women understood Hagar's flight, recognizing the questions from the angel of the Lord as theirs. These are questions with which womanist theologians wrestle. *Where are you coming from?* African American women have come from and through a multilayered landscape that continues to affect future directions. *Where are you going?* The constructed boundaries of race with gender and class continue to create endless issues and obstacles for future progress. There are the sticky floors of organizational and institutional structures that keep women of color at the lower rungs of the echelon. There are the glass ceilings that block advancement to only certain levels. There are the concrete ceilings that hide and obscure awareness of anything beyond the limited landscape in the current view. With those realizations, it is hard to know which way to go. Just as Hagar was offered no other option but to return to her mistress and submit to enslavement, so African American women have recognized their plight in similar terms. The inability to escape intersecting factors resulting from oppression and marginalization have felt at times like a command to return to the morass. But the good news was that African American women, like Hagar, recognized God as one who saw, heard, and heeded. And emboldened by such a God who is on their side, African American women realized a theological construction that sustained them.

Additionally, African American women saw Jesus as a Savior whose salvific power was for them. It was James Cone who boldly asserted that Jesus was the black Christ who provided the necessary soul for black liberation.[15] He believed there was need for a black theology that spoke to the needs of black people who suffered from white oppression. Jesus Christ was and is that liberator. Jesus was the incarnate God on the side of the oppressed. Cone's assertions were like those of Howard Thurman, who also noted Jesus was on the side of the disinherited and underprivileged. Yet, Cone had the temerity to suggest Jesus was the black Christ because he so sided with suffering black masses. Womanist theology promoted a similar construct viewing Jesus, the suffering servant, as one in divine solidarity with African American women. The biblical narrative affirmed that Jesus was in solidarity with those who are marginalized and oppressed and that he promoted a hierarchical restructuring which made the first last and the last first. Therefore, Jesus, siding with those who are the least in society, was an African American woman.[16]

At least that was Jacqueline Grant's assertion. In her opinion, womanist theology encompassed the threefold perspective of race, gender, and class, which Jesus embodied. First, as a Jew in first-century Palestine, Jesus was an oppressed racial minority. He could identify with the little people, which in the present context would include African American women, accepting them where they were. Second, Jesus' existence and example were not about male dominance but rather about the restoration of humanity. The fact that Jesus spoke to, included, and revealed himself to women indicates he was not simply a savior of men. Jesus died to save all of humanity. As Jarena Lee, the first African American woman officially sanctioned to preach in the AME Church, argued, "If the man may preach, because the Savior died for him, why not the woman? seeing that he died for her also."[17] Third, Jesus was poor and at the bottom of the socioeconomic ladder of his day. This too was the story for African American women. Because of the multiple oppressions under which African American women labor, "they are most often on the bottom of the social and economic ladder."[18] Yet, these marginalizing constructs were not the end because the resurrection of Jesus demonstrates the hope that the struggles of the present day are not eternal. Because Jesus was an overcomer, he provided hope that African American women could likewise overcome oppression. These beliefs engendered greater advocacy and agency. By joining the cause of Jesus Christ, African American women became servants of Christ, which meant standing against oppression wherever it was found. The result was that womanist theology enabled African American women to see themselves in a theological framework that simultaneously addressed confronting oppressions through the Godhead who saw, heard, and heeded by sending a Savior who was found in the experiences of African American women. Moreover, the perspective provided a praxis that informed how African American women lived into their faith. That place of praxis was the church, and African American women were the dominating force.

The Black Church

Daphne Wiggins demonstrated this fact in *Righteous Content: Black Women's Perspective of Church and Faith*. Her study of African American women considered their patterns of religiosity within the black church. The term "the black church" is used by Wiggins to refer to six historically independent and predominantly black denominations.[19] These were the churches whose roots and heritage were in the black community, established by people who had grown tired of being relegated to balcony seats and second-class status, wanting instead places where they could freely worship God. And wanting the freedom to form their own expression of church rooted in the African tradition, the black church emerged. Commonly, African Americans were either Methodists or Baptists because of the relative ease of establishing a church within those traditions. For Methodists, some churches were formed under primarily white denominations, while others belonged to one of the three predominantly black Methodist denominations—African Methodist Episcopal (AME), African Methodist Episcopal Zion (AMEZ), or Christian Methodist Episcopal (CME, formerly known as the Colored Methodist Episcopal Church).[20] In each of these denominations, churches were connectionally related with a presiding elder and a bishop who linked them to a larger judicatory structure. Baptist churches, believing in congregational polity and local church autonomy, were locally governed drawing upon the associational principles of church collaboration as determined by the needs of the congregation. Whether Baptist or Methodist, these black congregations constituted the center of the community, and while African American men and women, particularly in older generations, attended church, women closely resonated with the notion of being "raised in the church."

Being raised in the church certainly spoke to my experiences. Some of my earliest recollections are from church when I was a toddler in Sunday school classes. I distinctly remember standing on the chancel at the Church of God in Christ (COGIC) on St. Joseph Street in Elkhart, Indiana, where my great-uncle, Elder Norris Pierce Atkins Sr., was the pastor. It was Easter, and dressed in my Easter finest, wearing patent leather shoes, I delivered my "Easter piece." Later in my childhood, I remember singing in the children's choir at Chain Lake Baptist Church in Vandalia, Michigan, wearing one of the matching, blue polyester dresses that mothers made their daughters because the church did not have money for choir robes. I remember the days that started with Sunday school and transitioned to Sunday morning worship, afternoon dinner, and Sunday evening programs. Like many African American women of my generation and older, for me there were days when it seemed as though only church attendance was allowed. But the habits of worship were ingrained, so much so that at the age of sixteen, I used my newly gained driving liberty to attend church on Sunday mornings. Even during college years, Saturday night parties extending into the wee hours of the morning did not impact church attendance. I regularly left my dorm room early Sunday morning to attend worship services at Second Baptist Church in Bloomington, Indiana.

Did these experiences make me unique? No, they made me like many other African American women, because as Wiggins noted, there seemed to be an urgency regarding girls' participation in church. Boys enjoyed a greater range of activities in which they were allowed or encouraged to participate, while parents and guardians believed the church to be a more acceptable social outlet for girls.[21] These attitudes made church particularly female-friendly because church was organized to provide girls and young women with various activities in which they could be involved. Collectively, this female-friendly environment designed to provide acceptably social outlets created the normative foundation of church attendance for African American girls which translated into continued patterns of attendance through adulthood.

In addition, the church exposed African American women to an institutional context where the sacred space and experience was constituted primarily by women, which fostered female allegiance to the church.[22] Much of the experience of the black church was dominated by women. Sunday school classes, especially for children, were taught by women. The volunteer muscle that powered the work of the church was performed by women. Frequently choir directors and most of the choir members were women. I remember the nurses dressed in uniform and positioned at the back of the church were women. If someone "got happy,"[23] a cadre of nurses would spring to action, surrounding the member, waving fans, offering water, and using their strength to restrain so that no one was injured. And while the pastor and deacons were male, I also distinctly remember the female deaconesses, with lace doily–covered heads. They washed the hands of the pastor before he instituted the ordinance of communion. In that regard, I grew up believing that communion could not happen unless women uncovered the table and made everything ready for the Lord's Supper.

But it did not end there. Church dinners did not happen without the women. I never saw men frying chicken or fish or stirring up vats of potato salad or collard greens. The women of the church cooked, rivaling the quality of any restaurant. Furthermore, it was the women, armed with buckets and Murphy's Oil Soap, who cleaned the church. Pews would gleam in the Sunday morning sun, and the sanctuary stood in spotless splendor. Women served as members of standing committees such as Christian education, mission, and pastor's aid. By being so engaged in the work of the church, women came to see the church as theirs. They cared that the church was clean and well-kept. They cared that it was a welcoming space for families. Women took pride in bringing their best desserts to be shared at the church dinner. They did not mind giving themselves and their time to the church, and they conveyed these same affections and affinities to their daughters. It was the church, a space predominated by women, that fostered communal development for women. In fact, except for sororities and civic organizations such as the National Association of the Advancement for Colored People, no other black institution commands the kind of national scope or loyalty as the black church.[24]

The black church has also served as surrogate family, because it was the center of community for African American people, true especially from emancipation through reconstruction and into the great migration that motivated millions of African Americans to move to northern industrial cities. My maternal great-aunt shared that her family relocated from Mississippi to Gary, Indiana, as African Americans sought employment in the booming steel mills east of Chicago. Certainly, they relocated because of the jobs, but my great-aunt also desired to escape the violence that was the alleged cause of death of her father. Similarly, my paternal great-grandfather migrated from Obion, Tennessee, to Elkhart, Indiana, for work and to escape threatened attacks by the Ku Klux Klan. His son-in-law, my paternal grandfather, who also moved to Elkhart, gained employment with the railroad as a "shake out man," stoking the coal boilers of the train. Because these migrations, born of economic necessity, moved African Americans away from family and friends, the black church became the hub of activity for the community. The church was like family because so many were displaced. It was also a haven for people who found themselves as minorities, having lived in all-black communities, but migrating to white-dominated areas. The church was the place of worship, but it was also the place to network and connect with others. It was the home away from home for those who found themselves disconnected and isolated in new surroundings.

Women and the Black Church

This dependence on the church explains why it became so important for African American women. African American women left the south for northern urban areas, often finding some of the only opportunities open to them in the workforce were as domestics. "Between 1910 and 1940, almost three-fourths of all African American women were employed as domestic servants."[25] While northern jobs paid more than those in the south, the work remained soul-sapping and too often reminiscent of enslavement. African American women were hired for jobs that occupied the lowest strata of the labor force, meaning the positions were the most demeaning, dirtiest, and hazardous. Such work left women in need of restoration. Even women whose education provided pathways beyond menial labor were challenged in discriminatory environments that were oppressive and economically disenfranchising. For example, educator and civil rights activist Septima Clark described having 132 children in her two-teacher school, while the nearby white school had three children to one teacher.[26] In addition, teachers in Clark's school made $25.00 per week, while teachers in the white school made $85.00 per week. Facing such inequities in the workplace, African American women sought places of encouragement, and the black church provided stimulation and inspiration. Because the church was a nurturing, familial environment, it became the place in which African American women found solace. Older women provided wisdom and counsel. Peers became the sister friends with whom women bonded. Younger women became mentees who could be supported and promoted. Together, the women held one another, offering the kind of encouragement needed to persevere.

As women came together forming that bond of sisterhood, they recognized how best to pool their abilities for the needs of the community. Thus, the church became the launch pad from which women served in community. Women recognized the need to organize to protect themselves and develop their vocational skills, and the church was the means through which such organizing occurred. Church women organized clubs whose purpose was to work together in community to advocate for the rights of women and ensure racial progress. In fact, for many of these organizations, church membership was a prerequisite for belonging. And through these female-led, church-connected outreach efforts, necessary monetary support was raised and critical issues of advocacy were advanced. For example, black women's church organizations sent material aid to black war veterans and their families during and after the Civil War.[27] In the early twentieth century, church women raised money for numerous mission efforts, including education and benevolent assistance. And during the civil rights era, church women were instrumental in the Student Nonviolent Coordinating Council. Civil rights champion Ella Baker noted, "The movement of the fifties and sixties was carried largely by women, since it came out of the church groups . . . It's true that the number of women who carried the movement is much larger than that of the men."[28] With the strength of their network, African American church women became staunch advocates in their communities, seeing the work of the church as a natural extension of the mission work they were called to do. If Jesus Christ gave himself for the poor and oppressed, then they, being the hands and feet of Christ, needed to give themselves to others outside of the church.

Through the church and girded by faith, African American women came together to promote racial uplift, social reform, and advocacy. They saw themselves as people made in the image of God, and as they were affirmed in their faith, they sought to affirm others. Women saw a work that needed to be done and did it for the benefit of others, with the church—this female-dominated entity—serving as a primary delivery vehicle. As Nannie Helen Burroughs declared, "The Negro Church means the Negro woman . . . She carries the burdens of the church, and of the school and bears a great deal more than her economic share in the home."[29] And so carrying the burdens of the church, African American women assumed leadership roles. For example, a woman in Daphne Wiggins's study assumed the task of contacting absentee members to ensure that all was well.

In the Euro-American church tradition, this type of outreach was often assumed to be a pastoral duty, but in this black church context, the member believed the pastor's primary tasks were that of proclaiming the gospel and providing leadership.[30] Therefore, since absent member outreach was needed, she assumed responsibility for providing such leadership.

Significantly, by assuming leadership roles and associated tasks, African American women amassed a great deal of power in the black church. Women became church mothers, evangelists, missionaries, prayer band leaders, deaconesses, and teachers.[31] Church mothers were venerated elders in Baptist and Methodist churches, while in sanctified churches, Pentecostal and Holiness denominations, mothers were often the real power brokers of the church, with full authority within congregational and denominational structures.[32] In these traditions, women were appointed as leaders or overseers of women, and from these appointments, women established separate conventions and auxiliaries, wielding authority that at times rivaled or exceeded the impact and power of their churches. For example, Mother Lillian Brooks Coffey played a significant role in the Church of God in Christ. She was central to the history of the denomination, organizing the complex structure of the organization within the Women's Convention, and she engineered the Women's Convention's participation in larger black women's movements.[33] Pastors came to rely on the leadership of church mothers, seeking their counsel for matters in the church because these women knew the pulse of the church. The women knew whether a sermon resonated or if the hymn selection was moving and were quick to provide feedback. Additionally, women led as evangelists, inspiring the congregation as exhorters and serving as the "speaker," since women did not preach, during worship. Women were missionaries who raised funds for foreign aid, traveled to impoverished areas, or started schools to educate children and illiterate adults. In total, African American women assumed formal and informal roles of leadership, ensuring that the work of the church was accomplished.

The Backbone: Function or Position?

Because of these roles and the varied ways in which African American women moved the church forward, they were said to be the backbone of the black church. Not only did they lead and serve on committees and in auxiliaries, but also they filled the pews and attended the services. Women came to Sunday school, Sunday worship, prayer meeting, and Bible study. Commonly women brought family members along in tow. As the backbone provides support for the human body, making it possible for it to function and remain upright, so too did African American women provide that function in the black church.

Nevertheless, some argue that the characterization of women as the backbone of the church was not a positive one. Jacquelyn Grant has argued that "back" referred to position rather than function. What male ministers have meant more specifically was not that women were the backbone that allows the enterprise to function, but rather the ones who toiled in the background and that they should remain there merely as support workers.[34] Grant's argument is not without merit. Women dutifully served in the kitchen while men assumed the important leadership positions. Women financed the gospel with their hard-earned dollars only to turn monies over to male trustees to make financial decisions for the church. I have seen first ladies, the wives of male pastors, work as hard as the pastor without the recognition or compensation. In fact, some churches expect that "two in a box" benefit, believing that the female spouse of the male pastor should serve prominently as a volunteer in the life of the church. Grant called it a conspiracy that kept women relegated to background positions. Women, she contended, were rewarded for performing in background tasks but penalized for trying to move forward into leadership positions.[35] Such is the nature of the oppression that occurs for African American women in the black church.

At issue has been the unchallenged position of sexist practices in the black church. Of the historically African American denominations in the United States, all, according to Courtney Lyons of Baylor University, "decry racism as sin, yet *most* affirm patriarchy as biblical."[36] Texts such as "slaves obey your masters"[37] are met with theological and contextual refutations, while "women should be silent in the churches"[38] is declared as the gospel truth. In *Deacons in Today's Black Church*, Marvin McMickle baldly states, "The primary reason for excluding women [from church leadership] is gender discrimination."[39] And that discrimination is alive and well in too many churches. In 2012, I traveled with my husband to Georgia for my father in-law's funeral, in which I was asked to participate. As my husband and I prepared to be driven to the church, one of the church associate pastors literally ran down the street calling my name. "Rev. Jackson, Rev. Jackson!" he cried. And panting as he came alongside me, he said, "Now, we don't allow no women in the pulpit." When I arrived at the church, positioned at the foot of my father-in-law's casket was a lectern set aside for me.

Some faith traditions readily claim scriptural forbiddance as the justification barring the pulpit and pastoral ministry to women. However, Christine Smith, in *Beyond the Stained Glass Ceiling*, suggests that "power, sex, and ignorance are the major issues—rather than theology, Scripture, or gifts for ministry."[40] "Power concedes nothing without a demand," so said Frederick Douglass, and that truism holds regarding patriarchy in the church. To declare that "there is no longer male or female; for all of you are one in Christ Jesus"[41] is as biblical as "I permit no woman to teach or to have authority over a man; she is to keep silent."[42] However, a fully ensconced patriarchal power structure gives deference to the Scripture that maintains the patriarchal order. The biblical narrative is replete with women as prophets, judges, preachers, evangelists, apostles, gospel financiers, and deacons, but these realities have not swayed opinions. While women have assumed every leadership role in the black church, gender continues to function as a disqualifier for women's leadership by both African American women and men.

According to Ruth Brandon Minter, while women look to the male pastor figure to affirm them as women, men derive self-affirmation from male leadership because it allows them to assert manhood.

These preferences can be observed during Sunday worship. Because the pastor was esteemed as larger than life, carrying authoritative primacy in the black community, he was often the object of affection and fantasy for female congregants. Moreover, the greeting or touch of a pastor extended in the receiving line at the end of worship possibly served as the only male affirmation or contact received by a woman during the week. "This 'safe' male touch helped women to glow with a sense of self-worth and feel that they were still women."[43] Unwilling to relinquish such affirmations, women were said to prefer and even insist upon men as pastors. Considering the male point of view, as the preached word often dictated standards for right living, men were said to prefer hearing such commands from other men. To be admonished by women pastors created a power dynamic that resembled the relationship of a mother to her son, to which men objected. Additionally, as men recognized their minority status in the female-dominated church, the existence of the female pastor only served to reinforce their dispensability. Thus, these dynamics force both men and women to conspire consciously and unconsciously to retain pastoral patriarchy.

Female Leadership in the Black Church

What then of leadership opportunities for African American women in the black church? It is a source of real ambivalence. The black church continues to be a place of communal nurture with a great familial spirit that engenders connectivity. African American women can continue to find leadership development opportunities in the church, particularly in what could be labeled as entry-level roles. A constant need exists for leaders among children in the black church, particularly given a multigenerational trend where grandparents assume responsibility for the religious rearing of children whose parents no longer attend church. Nursery and Sunday school teachers, choir directors, as well as roles on the boards of Christian education or mission, abound. African American women not only will find the opportunities plentiful, but also they will find other women who are ready to help them become acclimated in these new roles. The black church continues to be that place where women are taken under wing and groomed to lead.

At issue, however, is the ability to ascend. A real and difficult-to-penetrate glass ceiling exists in the black church. One barrier is in the female-dominated roles. The leadership tenure in a traditionally female-dominated ministry of the black church is often measured in decades. For example, in the church that I serve, the chair of the board of missions has held that position for forty years. In a church that I previously served, the chair of the board of Christian education had served for more than twenty-five years. It is common that a woman will lead an auxiliary for so many years that the board is re-named for her after death. There is little opportunity for ascension and new leadership among younger women because the women leaders are firmly entrenched.

A second barrier is seen in male-dominated roles. Certain roles in the black church are controlled by men. The trustee ministry of the black church is often male-dominated. Harkening back to practices that asserted male control over financial issues, men traditionally oversee the collection, management, and distribution of money in the church. Then, quoting 1 Timothy 3:8-13, the black church has traditionally held that deacons must be men. I once argued with the pastor of a church who, objecting to the assertion that Phoebe was a deacon,[44] refused to have women as deacons. There was no real debate. He did not believe in the practice, and since he was the pastor, it was a settled matter. Even in churches where women are deacons, they are in the minority. Recent years have demonstrated a slow growth of female leadership in these traditionally male areas. However, that growth has been a result of exigency rather than an openness toward equality. As numbers have dwindled and fewer men participate in the life of the church, the insufficient numbers of available men have de-manded that women fill the leadership void.

But the most glaring barrier has been ascension to the pastoral office, and my story demonstrates the extent of the struggle African

American women in ministry have faced. Already I was an established and well-regarded leader in my church, the Emmanuel Baptist Church in Malden, Massachusetts, and the church enthusiastically affirmed my call to ministry and licensed me to preach. However, anticipating denominational objection to ordination, my pastor thought it prudent to direct me toward the American Baptist Churches USA (ABCUSA), a historically white but now minority-majority denomination, rather than the National Baptist Convention, USA, Inc., a historically African American denomination, for ordination. He recognized that the likelihood of an African American woman being called as pastor was much greater through an ABCUSA-affiliated church, because the denomination affirmed gender equality in pastoral leadership, where the National Baptists had no such stated policy. My pastor's mentorship was wise, as I was named the first African American and first woman to serve as senior pastor of the First Baptist Church in Needham, Massachusetts, a historic and predominantly Euro-American Baptist church. For the many joys and graces that I experienced as senior pastor, ministering in a cross-cultural context was difficult. The music was different; the worship experience was different; and the response to the sermonic moment was different. I taught my congregation to "talk back," saying "Praise the Lord" and "Amen" at appropriate times. But it was not the black church experience of my upbringing, and at some levels, I suffered spiritual dryness because I missed the familiar rhythms of my African American church culture.

After eight years of service, I was called to a denominational leadership position that required me to surrender my pulpit. Wanting to find a new church home in which I could serve, I spent more than a year visiting churches until I heard the Lord's confirmation. Through the leading of the Holy Spirit, I returned to the black church experience and my soul was watered. However, in exchange, I suffered as well because my leadership was stunted. While women comprise the majority of the church's congregation and function in numerous leadership roles, the pastoral pathways were partially obstructed. For example, the church was receptive to female pulpit associates serving as song or worship leaders and Scripture readers. However, when considering opportunities to lead corporate prayers or preach, there were noticeable gender inequities with male pulpit associates most frequently invited to serve in these capacities.

Such practices of limited inclusion lull the church into comfortable patterns of welcoming women into narrowed leadership opportunities while shrinking from full inclusion in other key areas. As a result, the congregation does not have the opportunity to experience true gender equality, instead seeing exception-based leadership where only select African American female clergy emerge to lead these male-dominated aspects of worship. In extreme instances, female pulpit associates sit on front pews, finely arrayed in their clergy apparel with no participating role in the worship. It is the worst kind of tokenism, as it marginalizes the leadership gifts of women. But such practices are marginalizing for the congregation as well. As churches look ahead to pastoral leadership transition, their vision is decidedly male-focused. Sanctioned sexism means that women are not recognized as viable candidates for senior pastorate roles.

New Paths for Leadership

Because the paths to ministerial leadership have been blocked for many African American women, they have forged creative paths to realize opportunities to serve. Researcher Eileen Campbell-Reed noted that 60 percent of the first wave of black female seminary graduates went to work in predominantly white mainline churches.[45] Notably, in the nearly two-decade timespan since Delores Carpenter's pioneering 2001 study about women's leadership in historic black churches, *Time for Honor: A Portrait of African American Clergywomen*, no other research-based, book-length multidenominational study about clergywomen in the US is presently available.[46] Yet we continue to see examples of African American women opting for pastorates through cross-cultural appointments and serving in contexts where they comprise the racial or ethnic minority. Nevertheless, in the present day and as a result of their longevity and success in these appointments, some women have been able to rise to the top of their religious traditions.

For example, Bishop LaTrelle Easterling, episcopal servant, is the first woman to lead the historic Baltimore-Washington Conference, the oldest and most diverse annual conference in the United Methodist Church. She was elevated to the episcopacy in July 2016 and appointed to head the Baltimore-Washington Conference in September 2016. She was one of four African American women and one Latina so elected in 2016. In 2018, the Evangelical Lutheran Church of American elected the first two African American clergywomen and the second Latina ever, as synod bishops.[47] Among the active bishops in the Episcopalian Church, five are African American women.

Similarly, some African American women sought standing and recognition in other denominations to serve as pastors, as I did. Delores Carpenter noted 45 percent of African American women clergy switched denominations in 1999, 24 percent of whom indicated that the change was ordination-related.[48] Rather than continuing in traditions with limited opportunities, African American women have turned to denominations that issued statements endorsing the ordination of women, such as the AME, AMEZ, and CME churches. In these traditions, district superintendents and bishops often placed women in pastoral positions, refusing to allow gender to function as a disqualifier. ABCUSA also issued resolutions that promoted and endorsed women in ministry. While the total numbers of women in ministry in ABCUSA have plateaued in the last twenty years with women comprising 13 percent of clergy and under 10 percent of pastors,[49] women constitute less than 1 percent of the pastors in historically African American Baptist churches.[50] By gaining standing in the ABCUSA, I realized and was provided opportunities that would have likely been denied to me in the black church.

The growth of women in ministry in the United Church of Christ and Unitarian Universalists suggest that women have found expanded opportunities in these traditions as well. According to the fall 2018 United Church of Christ Statistical Profile, approximately 50 percent of active, non-retired authorized ministers in the United Church of Christ identified as female.[51] Unitarian Universalist women comprise 57 percent of both ordained clergy and congregational pastors.[52]

African American women have also entered the academy to boost their opportunities for pastoral ministry. As women in general are less likely to benefit from the elevation that results from being regarded as an apprenticing Timothy to a wizened Paul, African American women have recognized that without credentialing, the obstacles blocking pastoral ministry are even greater. To that end in 2017, African American women comprised 26 percent of women pursuing the master of divinity degree and 30 percent of doctor of ministry students in seminaries accredited by the Association of Theological Schools (ATS).[53] Disregarding the old saying that intones "increase your learning, lose your burning," the trend for African American women enrolling in seminary continues to increase.

But more than that, exposure to the academy has served to open other opportunities as the doors to pastoral ministry have been barred in many places. Specifically, African American women are pursuing academic careers in greater numbers as a means of ministry. According to ATS 2017–2018 annual data, the total number of African American women serving as full-time faculty in ATS member seminaries rose from 93 to 100 from 2013 to 2017, which is a 7.5 percent increase.[54] While the increase is positive, the greatest growth in African American female appointments in seminaries and theological institutions is recognized at the level of assistant professors, which experienced a 40 percent increase from thirty assistant professors in 2013 to forty-two in 2014. Thus, African American women are making important inroads in higher education. An important disclaimer must be noted, however, because women in general are often stuck in lower-level academic positions. This sticky-floor, entry-level phenomenon can be seen with African American women pursuing tenure. The number of African American women associate professors at ATS schools remained fixed at 24 percent between 2013 and 2017 and dropped to 12.5 percent from twenty-four to twenty-one full professors in this same period. Faculty who do not achieve tenure within the institution's specified timeframe are left to seek appointments at other institutions, often at the assistant professor level, in hopes of achieving tenure elsewhere.

It also bears noting that the pursuit of the doctor of ministry degree presents challenges as well. The doctor of ministry degree identifies the holder as an expert ministry practitioner. However, because women have often been barred from tangible ministry practice, the designation of expert is diminished. Additionally, the doctor of ministry is not universally respected in the academy because it is believed to lack academic rigor. I once heard seminary faculty demean the doctor of ministry degree, claiming that recipients were most interested in the title of "doctor" over academic achievement. Such attitudes affect women more so than men because they are the ones less likely to be regarded as practitioners, due to the lack of ministerial experience, or academic theorists revered for their scholarly achievements. These combined impacts may also explain the dearth of women in top-level leadership positions in the academy. Because top-level faculty rank is often a prerequisite for advancement into leadership, women are missing out on career opportunities.[55]

Remaining steadfast in pursuit of their call to ministry, African American women have alternatively engaged in specialized ministries and nonprofit management, leveraging their skills in broad ways. Such breadth is possible in part because African American clergy have been historically required to be more than spiritual leaders. Given the needs of their communities, clergy typically see their roles more holistically, fulfilling vital roles of leading their community and accessing goods and services necessary to meet the social and political needs of their constituents.[56] Such diverse experiences have helped prepare African American women to pursue these rapidly growing ministerial paths. The ability to listen to the needs of others and serve as a pastoral presence have positioned African American women for chaplaincy and spiritual direction. Skills in community organizing have opened doors to service leadership positions. In addition, certification programs which provide the necessary credentialing for specialized roles are less expensive than a seminary degree, making these paths to ministry more attractive.

The number of African American women deploying their theological training in nonprofit leadership is also increasing. In general, the nonprofit sector espouses a meritocratic ideal regarding leadership and leadership opportunities, with an assumption that anyone can advance with sufficient effort.[57] In addition, the number of organizations whose identity is based on being dedicated to people of color or immigrants have created more space for African Americans leadership, as more people of color are inclined to apply for these positions. These promises for advancement and opportunity have encouraged African American women to step forward. In fact, according to the Nonprofits, Leadership, and Race survey conducted by the Building Movement Project in 2017, people of color are more likely to be interested in becoming a nonprofit leader than whites.[58] Interest has not been enough to ensure leadership opportunities for African American women. As has been seen in pastoral ministry, African American women have struggled to break into nonprofit leadership opportunities as well, noting that they are passed over for new jobs or overlooked for promotions, face assumptions that they are underqualified and inexperienced in comparison with white and/or male colleagues, or are stereotyped as being overly aggressive or "angry."[59]

Tired of being blocked and barred, African American women have also sought to establish their own churches. Having had the privilege of serving as a thought leader of the 2018 Lott Carey Pilgrimage of Striving and Thriving for women in ministry, I was surprised that nearly half of the twenty-five-member cohort had planted their own churches. A plausible precedent for this work was recognized through the Church of God in Christ and its functioning in the early twentieth century. Church planting was accepted as women's work, with women assuming the responsibilities of drawing in congregants to establish or "dig out" a church for a male to pastor.[60] Specifically, women would convene tent meetings or engage in street evangelism, and when a critical mass of converts was formed, a letter was mailed to the denominational body requesting that a male pastor be sent. Ironically the Church of God in Christ does not recognize the ordination of women, but the practice of women planting churches has been appropriated by other traditions, paving the way for female planted and led churches.

Of course, many African American women have remained in the churches and denominations that nurtured them, obstacles notwithstanding. African American women suffer multiple oppressions; however, they see themselves first as people of color. Therefore, their primary efforts have been devoted to lifting people of African ancestry and creating community. Because the black church has been the central feature of the black community and wanting to ensure preservation, African American women have placed themselves in secondary positions for the benefit of others. Then, believing with Hagar that God indeed sees, hears, and heeds, African American women held fast to Proverbs 18:16, "A gift opens doors; it gives access to the great." As African American women used their God-given talents, those talents have enabled them to excel. I am reminded of Rev. Dr. Prathia Hall whose 1962 prayer, featuring the spontaneous and rhythmic utterance of "I Have a Dream," was purportedly heard, adopted, and made famous by Martin Luther King Jr. He was later quoted as saying, "Prathia Hall is the one platform speaker I would prefer not to follow."[61] Hall's gifts made room for her and, as evidenced by King's praise, she was recognized by one of the greatest orators of the twentieth century. In other words, her gifts gave access to the great. But exhibiting a humility that is characteristic of womanist leadership, she eschewed credit. In an interview, Hall said that if she did have a part in King's use of the phrase she was "greatly honored" and that King "did more with it than I could have done."[62]

Hall's story reminds us that God has used African American women to lead in the church. While sexism has been tolerated and patriarchy permitted to function unchecked, God has seen, heard, and heeded in ways that made space for African American women to lead. Through their leadership the black church has grown and been sustained. These examples persuade me to believe that leadership opportunities will increase as African American women continue to exercise their gifts. Led by a spirit that encourages some to press for change within patriarchal structures, some to move to new structures, and some to create their own, God is moving. And it makes sense for, after all, God is on our side.

Lessons in Womanist Leadership

■ Exercise faith by sight. African American women recognized God as on their side and a Savior, Jesus Christ, who represented them not in his maleness but as one who cared chiefly about the oppressed and poor. When you see yourself in the faith narrative, you are more likely to remain committed.

■ Realize faith formation through the church. The church provided and continues to provide a vehicle for community and connectivity for African American women, through which they can exercise their gifts of leadership.

■ Find new paths to leadership. The sanctioned sexism of the church has moved women to seek informal and formal new paths to realize ministerial leadership. You do not have to remain stuck because expanded opportunities are opening.

■ Focus on your gifts. African American women embrace the proverb that one's gifts will make room for them.

Notes

1. David Masci, "Five Facts about the Religious Lives of African Americans," Pew Research Center, February 7, 2018, https://www.pewresearch.org/fact-tank/2018/02/07/5-facts-about-the-religious-lives-of-african-americans/, accessed May 30, 2019.

2. Courtney Lyons, "Breaking Through the Extra-Thick Stained-Glass Ceiling: African American Baptist Women in Ministry," *Review & Expositor* 110, no. 1 (Winter 2013), 79.

3. William B. McClain in *Songs of Zion* (Nashville: Abingdon, 1981), ix.

4. Arthur C. Jones, *Wade in the Water: The Wisdom of the Spiritual* (Maryknoll, NY: Orbis Books, 1993), 24.

5. Howard Thurman, *Jesus and the Disinherited* (1976; Boston: Beacon Press, 2012), 30.

6. Ibid., 31.

7. James H. Evans Jr., *We Have Been Believers: An African American Systematic Theology* (Minneapolis: Fortress Press, 1992), 40–41.

8. Gayraud S. Wilmore, *Black Religion and Black Radicalism*, 2nd ed. (1973; Maryknoll, NY: Orbis Books, 1983), 121.

9. 2 Kings 19:9.

10. Genesis 9:22-27.

11. Luke 4:18.

12. Evans, 97–98.

13. Pew Research Center, Religion and Public Life, "A Religious Portrait of African-Americans," Appendix: Detailed Tables, http://www.pewresearch.org/wp-content/uploads/sites/7/2009/01/appendix.pdf, accessed January 17, 2019.

14. Stephanie V. Mitchem, *Introducing Womanist Theology* (Maryknoll, NY: Orbis Books, 2002), 23.

15. Wilmore, 218.

16. Jacqueline Grant, *White Woman's Christ and Black Woman's Jesus: Feminist Christology and Womanist Response* (Atlanta: Scholars Press, 1989), 220.

17. Jarena Lee, *Religious Experience and Journal of Mrs. Jarena Lee* (Philadelphia: n.p., 1836), 11.

18. Grant, 210.

19. Daphne C. Wiggins, *Righteous Content: Black Women's Perspectives of Church and Faith* (New York: New York University Press, 2005), 203. Churches included are the African Methodist Episcopal Church, African Methodist Episcopal Zion Church, Christian Methodist Episcopal Church, National Baptist Convention, USA, Inc., National Baptist Convention, and Church of God in Christ.

20. Theresa Hoover, "Black Women and the Churches," in *Black Theology: A Documentary History*, vol. 1: *1966–1979*, ed. James H. Cone and Gayraud S. Wilmore, 2nd ed. (1979; Maryknoll, NY: Orbis Books, 2005), 296.

21. Wiggins, 31–32.

22. Ibid., 30.

23. To "get happy," also known as being slain in the spirit, is a term used in Pentecostal and charismatic traditions. It refers to the ecstatic manifestation of the Holy Spirit where those under the Spirit's influence experience uncontrollable emotional responses which can include, but are not limited to, speaking in tongues, dancing, crying, or fainting.

24. Wiggins, 30.

25. Bettye Collier-Thomas, *Jesus, Jobs, and Justice: African American Women and Religion* (New York: Alfred A. Knopf, 2010), 281.

26. Grace Jordan McFadden, "Septima P. Clark and the Struggle for Human Rights," in *Women in the Civil Rights Movement: Trailblazers and Torchbearers, 1941–1965*, ed. Vicki L. Crawford, Jacqueline Anne Rouse, and Barbara Woods (Bloomington: Indiana University Press, 1993), 86.

27. Paula Giddings, *When and Where I Enter: The Impact of Black Women on Race and Sex in America* (New York: HarperCollins, 1984), 72.

28. Ibid., 284.

29. Collier-Thomas, 59.

30. Wiggins, 38.

31. Cheryl Townsend Gilkes, *If It Wasn't for the Women—: Black Women's Experience and Womanist Culture in Church and Community* (Maryknoll, NY: Orbis Books, 2001), 46.

32. Ibid., 68.

33. Ibid., 124.

34. Jacquelyn Grant, "Black Theology and the Black Woman," in *Black Theology: A Documentary History*, vol. 1: *1966–1979*, ed. James H. Cone and Gayraud S. Wilmore, 2nd ed. (1979; Maryknoll, NY: Orbis Books, 2005), 328.

35. Ibid.

36. Lyons, 78.

37. Ephesians 6:5.

38. 1 Corinthians 14:34.

39. McMickle is quoted in Lyons, 88.

40. Christine Smith, *Beyond the Stained Glass Ceiling: Equipping and Encouraging Female Pastors* (Valley Forge, PA: Judson Press, 2013), 36.

41. Galatians 3:28.

42. 1 Timothy 2:12.

43. Ruth Brandon Minter, "Hidden Dynamics Block Women's Access to Pulpits," Religion Online, https://www.religion-online.org/article/hidden-dynamics-block-womens-access-to-pulpits/, accessed November 25, 2018.

44. Romans 16:1.

45. Eileen Campbell-Reed, *The State of Clergywomen in the United States: A Statistical Update*, October 2018, 8.

46. Ibid., 3.

47. Ibid., 8.

48. Delores C. Carpenter, *A Time for Honor: A Portrait of African American Clergywomen* (St. Louis, MO: Chalice Press, 2001), 139–40.

49. Campbell-Reed, 8.

50. Lyons, 79.

51. United Church of Christ Statistical Profile, fall 2018, 24.

52. Campbell-Reed, 6.

53. ATS Data Tables 2017–2018 Appendices, 43.

54. Ibid., 77.

55. Pamela L. Eddy and Kelly Ward, "Problematizing Gender in Higher Education: Why Leaning In Isn't Enough," in *Critical Approaches to Women and Gender in Higher Education*, ed. Pamela L. Eddy, Kelly Ward, and Tehmina Khwaja (New York: Palmgrave Macmillan, 2017), 14.

56. Kirkpatrick G. Cohall and Bruce S. Cooper, "Educating American Baptist Pastors: A National Survey of Church Leaders," *Journal of Research on Christian Education* 19, no. 1 (2010), 52.

57. Ofronama Biu, "Race to Lead: Women of Color in the Nonprofit Sector," Building Movement Project, February 2019, 7.

58. Sean Thomas-Breitfeld and Frances Kunreuther, "Race to Lead: Confronting the Nonprofit Racial Leadership Gap," Building Movement Project, February 2019, 2.

59. Biu, 21–22.

60. Anthea D. Butler, *Women in the Church of God in Christ: Making a Sanctified World* (Chapel Hill: University of North Carolina Press, 2007), 49.

61. PBS, This Far by Faith, "People of Faith: Prathia Hall," http://www.pbs.org/thisfarbyfaith/people/prathia_hall.html, accessed January 21, 2019.

62. Drew D. Hansen, *The Dream: Martin Luther King Jr. and the Speech That Inspired a Nation* (New York: Ecco, 2003), 250.

CHAPTER 4

Pardon My Blackness, I Didn't Mean to Shine

"Pardon my blackness, I didn't mean to shine." I grew up hearing this phrase from my parents. It stemmed from their collegiate days at Indiana University. Being first-generation college students, as my parents were, many African American students matriculating in the 1960s shouldered the responsibility to do well in school. They worked hard and felt pride when their efforts paid off. However, doing well did not guarantee recognition. There were the occasions when acing a test or performing well in a class received no acknowledgment from faculty. As a result, African American students became one another's support system. They cheered one another when someone did well and offered fanfare particularly because it was withheld from others. And the common refrain of celebration and acknowledgment for these collegiate students became, "Pardon my blackness, I didn't mean to shine." But what does this mean?

Part of the answer is found in understanding the use of grease. As early as 1699, explorers to the African continent documented that African people would apply grease to their bodies. Explorer William Dampier, in *A New Voyage Around the World*, noted how Africans used various oils and grease on their bodies to clog pores as a means of disease prevention and as a beauty practice.[1] In 1759, Swedish botanist and zoologist Carl Linnaeus updated his biological classification in *Systema naturae*, describing the African as one who "*Anoints* himself with grease."[2] At issue for these explorers was what seemed to them to be a confusing practice. Why would people apply animal fat to their bodies? Ironically, use of oils and animal grease was common in eighteenth-century English perfumeries. However, the technologies used by these manufacturers were said to purify bear

grease as it was clarified and perfumed.[3] Thus it was not the Africans'
application of the grease that was at issue, but rather the basal stink
associated with "raw" animal grease. As such, use of grease became
one reason, among many, for discrimination toward Africans because
they were said to smell badly.

Nevertheless, these practices were used with grease being applied
for many purposes. Instead of the palm oil used in Africa for hair-
dressing, black slaves were said to use bacon grease or butter to
condition and soften hair, as well as to make it shine.[4] The use of
oil or grease also gave the hair a straighter appearance. Grease was
thought to ward off bugs and other pests while sleeping. The application of grease was a custom of most people in hot countries,
as grease defended their skins from the scorching heat of the sun.[5]
African cultures engaged in the daily application of oils and grease
as ministration for dry skin hundreds of years before modern science affirmed its use.[6] Having applied grease as a common multi-
purposed remedy, people of African descent would "shine" with
an oily appearance.

The association of the word "shine" with the potentially oily appearance of African people was not the only connotation of the idiom,
however. In 1910, Ford Dabney and Cecil Mack penned the lyrics to
a ragtime song called "That's Why They Call Me Shine." The lyrics
suggested a singer who was black. The happy-go-lucky attitude, smil-
ing mouth with white pearly teeth, and shady color, not to mention
curly hair, served as confirming characteristics for a person of African
ancestry who also fit the common stereotypes of the day. At the same
time, however, as African American boys and men were employed as
shoe shiners, "shine" became a derogatory name affixed to such la-
borers. Thus, regardless of appearance, outward persona, or employment, to be called a "shine" was an undeniably racist slur levied
against African Americans.

So, to shine harkened to the early explorers' observation of African
people and to the derogatory terms applied to African American people, men specifically. Yet like much that was developed for harm,

African Americans subverted those meanings to represent good. Rather than accept the negative connotations, to shine was redefined and likened to Jesus' words as recorded in Matthew 5:15-16: "No one after lighting a lamp puts it under the bushel basket, but on the lampstand, and it gives light to all in the house. In the same way, let your light shine before others, so that they may see your good works and give glory to your Father in heaven." To shine, as such, means to allow the light of God given to us through Jesus Christ to shine through us so that others would see that light in us. Shining allows others to see our brilliance, potential, and intelligence. Therefore, to say, "Pardon my blackness, I didn't mean to shine," was a tongue-in-cheek way of saying, "I may be black, but look at my God-given brilliance." These collegiate students were using the phrase to lift and encourage one another. And having that sense of self-esteem was an important attribute to cultivate for the young students of my parents' day, because not everyone recognized or affirmed the brilliance of African American students.

My mother told of a storied professor of nutrition at Indiana University in the 1960s. Students shied away from this professor because she was known for being particularly challenging where grades were concerned. However, those majoring in elementary education, physical education, and health were required to take her classes. Because the instructor was fond of Scantron test forms, students taking tests in her classes rarely received results; only a letter grade. As the relatively small cohort of African American students who had to take her class learned, the letter grade always given to African American students was C.

One day, one student went to the professor's desk to ask her a question. Noticing that the professor's grade book was open, the student saw her name listed with a middle initial of C. When the student said, "Excuse me, professor, but my middle initial is not C," the student was told to mind her own business. Before the professor closed the grade book, the student noticed other African American classmates' names on the roster as well. Each student had the middle initial of C.

As they conferred at the end of the semester, each of these African American students had received a final grade of C.

That letter C stood for "colored." In this professor's opinion, African American students were not capable of achieving a higher grade. Her built-in bias ensured that her opinion remained unchanged. This is only one example of the challenges African Americans have had in the quest to be received as academically equal. Theories of black inferiority have manifested since the first European explorers came to Africa. Such theories persisted as part of the rationale for enslavement: specifically, that people of African ancestry were mentally childlike and thus enslavement was paternalistic and benevolent. Because of such theories, black parents for generations have instilled in their children that "you have to be twice as good to get half as far." African American children have been clearly given this message and mandate for academic excellence. But I dare say the challenge of the mandate fell more so to African American women and girls because the intersection of gender and racial biases typically positions African American women at the bottom of social and professional hierarchies. To overcome these stereotypes and shine, African American women turned to education.

Public Intellectuals to Advance the Race

As Pauline Hopkins noted in *Colored American Magazine*, "From the time that the first importation of Africans began to add comfort and wealth to the existence of the New World Community, the Negro woman has been constantly proving the intellectual character of her race in unexpected directions."[7] Mid-eighteenth-century philosophers created a theory of the black African's status that cemented prejudicial beliefs. Their assumption was that the black African had degenerated from a white prototype such that nerves, brains, and capacity to reason were altered.[8] Because of their supposed lack of intellect and subordinated status within the human species, the only role for the African was to "toil for white masters."[9] It was an aspersion cast upon the entire race, and as a result, African

American people in general but women specifically did not have the luxury of an individualized focus where intelligence was concerned. Since the entire race of people were considered intellectually challenged, African American women found it necessary to advocate for all to shape public discourse against racially biased attitudes. Women surmised that if African Americans were more favorably regarded at a higher standard through the realization of middle-class, Protestant values, the entire race of people would benefit, and African American people as a whole would be better-received. It was a lofty if not naïve goal, but it was born of a realization that discrimination reduced the entire race to the most debased characterizations and stereotypes of black people.

The women's club movement became one of the vehicles through which this work of positive racial promotion was undertaken. The most prominent of the national clubs was the National Association of Colored Women (NACW), established in 1896. NACW women saw themselves as willing educators of public opinion. They called themselves the "real new woman in American life" because of their progressive role and stance in all arenas of life: home, church, club, and in community.[10] Club women, assuming the mantle of public intellectuals, worked to change old ideas bound in white people's impression of African Americans. Through their discourses, they sought to demonstrate that it was not aptitude that shackled the African American, but opportunity. Club women used their intellectualism to refute the subservient claims of a woman's place and worth. And they shifted public opinion by voicing their beliefs in the public square.

These public pronouncements were the height of unorthodoxy in the late nineteenth and early twentieth centuries. The work of changing societal perceptions required African American women to engage in public discourse, and yet, such practices were not acceptable for women. Respectability, a theorized operational norm, espoused middle-class standards that dictated a woman's realm was the home. To that end, the most progressive abolitionist newspaper in 1832 counseled, "The voice of woman should not be heard in public debates, but there are other ways in which her influence would be beneficial."[11] While decades had passed between this published sentiment and the heyday of the club movement, these views regarding a woman's place being the private sphere remained largely unchanged. For African American women, the paradox was real. On one hand, leading women were encouraging their race to adopt these middle-class values of decorum and respectability, with an expectation that women would marry, raise children, and work within the home. If women functioned outside of the home, their roles should be limited to volunteering through church or women's club service with involvement emphasizing social graces, culture, and refinement. These same middle-class values created expectations for African American men as well. They were expected to serve as the primary breadwinners of the home and the source of economic security for the family. By functioning in these societally defined roles, black families could possibly ascend to the middle class and attain a measure of social acceptability.

However, on the other hand, these expectations proved to be too confining in practice. During enslavement, African American women had had to work equally with their male counterparts, and this need did not change during the postbellum period. It was largely an issue of economics. African American families could not survive on a single wage earner's income in the household. Although women were largely employed in low-wage positions such as domestics or washerwomen, their salaries helped to make ends meet, especially as African American men struggled to assert dominance in the employment ranks. Equally important was the realization by African American women that they needed to educate and advance themselves so that they might advance others. This sentiment was expressed in the motto of the NACW, which stressed "lifting as we climb." Women leaders insisted upon a foundation of moral fortitude in hopes of gaining respectability for African American people, which was evidenced by club work focused on strengthening women, the home, and family. And even though a focus on respectability suggested a private persona rather than public pronouncements, women could not afford to be limited. However, acting in such unorthodox ways came at a cost.

At issue was the fact that women who were engaged in public discourse were viewed as sexually promiscuous because they would dare to operate in the public sphere. Only prostitutes were so publicly exposed. Yet many of the emergent African American women leaders, functioning as public intellectuals, felt compelled to advocate for the betterment of African American people. These women decided they could not be concerned with the negative stigmas affixed to their public protests. They became some of the most prolific writers, speakers, and intellectual thinkers of the late nineteenth and early twentieth centuries who boldly used their influence to change the perceptions of society, while demonstrating that a woman's place was wherever she was needed. Additionally, they leveraged their intellectual abilities to lift others, allowing their lights to shine so that all could see.

Women Who Shined

A notable champion of civil rights, woman's suffrage, and racial uplift, Mary Church Terrell stands as a shining example. Born in Memphis, Tennessee, in 1863, Mary Church was the child of Robert and Louise Ayers Church, who were formerly enslaved and yet had become prominent business people. Their success provided their daughter with educational opportunities from an early age. She attended Oberlin College opting to pursue the "gentleman's course" of study, which included learning classical Latin and Greek. Her academic pursuits were a point of contention for her friends, who suggested that such study would decrease her chances of marriage.[12] Ignoring the protestations, Mary earned a bachelor of arts in 1884, and a master of arts, also from Oberlin, in 1888. Mary taught at Wilberforce University, a decision to which her father was vehemently opposed. Believing a lady of her standing should not work, Robert Church was unhappy enough to disinherit his daughter, and he refused to write to her for a year because she chose a career after graduation.[13] After two years, Mary relocated to

Washington, DC, where she was a teacher of languages at the Colored High School for one year.

In 1889, Mary traveled and studied in Europe, where she became fluent in French, German, and Italian. She demonstrated her dexterity for language, having been invited to speak at the International Congress of Women held in Berlin in 1904, by delivering her remarks in German, French, and English.[14] Returning from Europe, she resumed her position at the Colored High School, and in 1891, at the ripe old age of twenty-eight, she married Robert Terrell, the Latin Department head and a Harvard-educated lawyer who would later be appointed to serve as a judge in Washington, DC.

Mary Church Terrell was one of the wealthiest and most educated African American woman of her time, and yet she recognized that "racist white America . . . would not allow an educated, rich black woman to be treated with the same respect as any white American woman."[15] In short, Terrell concluded that the world would always judge black people by the color of their skin regardless of personal achievement. Those who might claim ascension or advancement based on educational attainment or net worth remained inextricably bound to those who were uneducated and impoverished based on pigmentation. As Terrell noted, "Self-preservation demands that [black women] go among the lowly, illiterate and even the vicious, to whom they are bound by ties of race and sex . . . to reclaim them."[16] For her, this was the only way to truly gain respectability: the entire race had to rise together.

These sentiments—the need for racial uplift and the belief that educated African American women carried a primary responsibility for the burden of lifting—inspired many women to begin schools to train attendees. Lucy C. Laney established the Haines Normal and Industrial Institute in Augusta, Georgia, in 1886. Blaming the institution of slavery for creating an ignorant people who would be prejudged by the crippling effects of enslavement, Laney saw it as the educated black woman's burden to address these ills. Women were needed as educators in the home, but more than that, women were needed as educators in society. "The educated Negro woman, the woman of character and culture, is needed in the schoolroom not only in the kindergarten, and in the primary and the secondary school; but she is needed in high school, the academy, and the college."[17]

Nannie Helen Burroughs founded the National Training School for Girls in Washington, DC. Approaching this burden carried by African American women both academically and vocationally, Burroughs sought to train women in domestic services. She believed that as domestic services were professionalized, African American women would be better positioned to obtain higher-paid, standardized professions of the future.[18] Charlotte Hawkins Brown established the Palmer Memorial Institute. Her school was expressly created to overcome a common stereotype that African Americans were innately inferior to whites and did not need any schooling beyond vocational training.

More commonly, however, is the fact we do not know the African American women who led by promoting education as the focus. The NACW is a prime example of this fact. The history of the organization as chronicled by Elizabeth Davis reveals a largely anonymous roster of women. The NACW was the largest and arguably most important African American women's club of the early twentieth century, but the organization and many of its leaders remain obscure. One of the organization's most well-known presidents was Margaret Murray Washington, a leader whom Davis lists simply as Mrs. Booker T. Washington because of her famous husband. Womanist and feminist scholars may recognize the names of Mary Church Terrell, Josephine Silone Yates, and Hallie Quinn Brown, but few outside such academic circles would know these women. Mary McLeod Bethune was a past president of NACW, but she is better-known from her work with the United Council of Negro Women, her appointment to the federal government by Franklin D. Roosevelt, and as the founder of the Daytona School for Girls, which later became Bethune-Cookman University. The point is that Bethune may have been known in some circles, but the women in the organization that she helped to lead were largely unknown because the leaders were not seeking fame or recognition. They were trying to make a difference by promoting the need for education.

Education as the Key

The experiences of public intellectuals and the club movement solidified the notion that education was the key means of advancement. Such awareness was particularly important as African Americans began migrating to the north in the early twentieth century, where the hope of education was to provide better job opportunities. Wanting to escape the discrimination and disenfranchisement in the south, African Americans fled from southern states as Jim Crow laws were implemented to codify discriminatory practices. However, African Americans found themselves relegated to the most menial jobs. For women, this meant low-wage and low-status employment as domestics or washerwomen, work in which they were subject to unwanted advances and sexual exploitation by men who regarded these women as "morally loose."[19] In fact, rape was a common occurrence. Feeling powerless against the abuses, African American parents believed that education would enable their daughters to escape this trap. Through education, women could realize greater opportunities beyond that of domestic service. Additionally, there was a greater hope and expectation that educated women would use their education to help others, breaking a cycle of abuse and exploitation. This expectation further perpetuated a cultural mindset that women were responsible for both education and uplift.

In the twentieth century, African American women focused their educational pursuits on formalized academic study. The years after World War II demonstrated that African American women were attending colleges at rates higher than white women or African American men. By 1952–1953, African American women received 62.4 percent of all degrees from historically black colleges.[20] And these trends have continued into the twenty-first century. According to the *Journal of Blacks in Higher Education*, African American women currently earn two-thirds of all African American bachelor's degrees, 70 percent of all master's degrees, and more than 60 percent of all doctorates.[21]

This focus on formalized study served to create expanded vocational and professional opportunities, and teaching became the first profession opened to African Americans. It was an attractive vocational choice because through teaching, African American women gained respectability and were able escape from the limitations society imposed on them.[22] According to some estimates, the teaching profession attracted 90 percent of educated black women in the half century following emancipation.[23] So many women could pursue careers as teachers because it was a profession in high demand. There was always the perceived need for people to educate "masses of ignorant Negroes."[24] But this racist attitude was also a motivation to pursue the profession. By successfully educating African American students, teachers helped to subvert negative stigmas, demonstrating that African American people were capable of academic achievement.

But African Americans women did not limit themselves in their professional vocations. Because opportunities have opened greatly in the latter quarter of the twentieth century, choices have expanded beyond the education professions. African American women have distinguished themselves as leaders in every field of endeavor because of their high rates of academic credentialing. As one who completed advanced study in the science, technology, engineering, and math (STEM) fields, I recognize the importance of women of color assuming leadership roles in these fields so that others might follow. It is how African American women have demonstrated leadership in education as trailblazers and role models. As African American women continue to significantly outnumber African American men at the highest-ranked universities, a spillover effect will be seen in graduate school, professional positions, and leadership posts in our society.[25]

Education Begins at Home

African American women have also modeled leadership by providing education through home training, which prepares children to be successful in the world. Like many parents, I have shared with my African American teenage son that people will judge him by the color of his skin. He may not have an opportunity to open his mouth to demonstrate that he is educated before opinions are set. The pre-judged mindset will attempt to relegate him to the lowest level of acceptability. One look at his dreadlocked hairstyle and slouchy clothing would cause some people to associate him with a criminal element rather than being an average male teen. And because of this, I am focused on education—an education that started with home training and continues with the emphasis of academic advancement.

Home training continues to be stressed in the African American family and particularly by women to ensure that their children learn dignified behavior. Aspects of home training include learning how to speak only when spoken to, referring to adults using honorific titles to show respect, and saying "please" and "thank you" to demonstrate proper manners. Again, it harkens back to postbellum periods when African Americans sought respectability from the dominant culture. If individual African Americans could exhibit a basic level of decorum, all members of the race would be regarded at a higher level of acceptability. As such, my paternal grandmother, a descendent from enslaved parents, insisted on cleanliness and punctuality as part of her children's home training. To her, there was no excuse for being unkempt or late.

Part of my home training consisted of what is most commonly referred to as elocution. My mother often corrected my articulation. It was incredibly frustrating as a child to have stories constantly interrupted by linguistic adjustments: subject and verb agreement; proper conjugation and use of pronouns; and Midwestern dialectical pronunciations. She eschewed the idea that we were "talking white"; rather, we were speaking proper English, which for her was a requirement.

These are lessons that I now pass on to my child with the same level of insistence, while laboring under the sad reality of the continuing need. I remember being congratulated by a store clerk when my son confidently made a purchase while engaging her in conversation. Of course, I have parental pride that my child is well-spoken, but does being congratulated suggest his abilities to be incongruent with the expectations that some have of an African American teenager? If so, the lessons continue to be significant and necessary. This example typifies why African American parents continue to instill in their children that they must be twice as good as a white person to receive the same level of respect, opportunity, or status. It explains why African American families continue to stress education for their children with ever-increasing expectations for advancement. The societal propensity to negatively prejudge African Americans requires a sustained focus on education.

Advocacy is also a critical requirement as parents educate their children. African American mothers who participated in a research study of families who raised academically successful African American young women noted that they encouraged their daughters "to believe they can achieve as much as anyone and not to listen to racial stereotyping that Blacks are not as competent."[26] The study confirms that African American women continue to promote a model of academic advancement through individual achievement, expansion into advanced vocational professions, and advocacy that begins in the home with extension into the community.

These strategies constitute ways that African American women lead in their homes and communities, as they help shape competent and capable individuals. Because of enslavement, there was an incredible need for and effort required to educate in every way a people who had been suppressed and intentionally untaught. Under slavery, African Americans were not educated to understand or appreciate homemaking or functioning in family units. Most people were unable to read or write. Some were inarticulate or hampered in the ability to communicate, speaking only broken patois. There was no economic acuity and no means to earn a living other than servitude. Every aspect of educational exposure was required. African culture had taught these values and societal norms, but enslavement stripped them all away. Thus, when emancipation freed millions of people, it left them without resources or means to improve their situations. As such, African American men and woman, those who were recognized as the leaders of the educational movement during reconstruction and into the twentieth century, all worked to ensure uplift. But, given the ways that African American women were marginalized, they had to challenge convention to ensure progression.

Overcoming to Lead

As we reflect on the stories of public intellectuals and their focus on respectability and insistence on education, we gain insights on how African American women lead. They overcame oppressive systems by using their voices, gained through home training or formalized instruction, remaining determined to realize better for themselves and others. Specifically, African American women were unbowed to the conventions of patriarchy. A patriarchal system of hierarchy operates to suppress and ultimately silence those who are deemed subordinate. Raising one's social status in the hierarchy is predicated on functioning within the accepted norms of those in power. However, African American women refused to fall in line. Although they occupied the lowest rung on the social ladder, African American women led from the bottom by speaking up and speaking out. Their vocal advocacy worked against the defined order of patriarchy, since women were supposed to be silent. Without regard to convention, many of these women spoke publicly and wrote passionately, weathering negative stigmas. To that end, societal pressures were used as tactics designed to silence women. African American female intellectuals were labeled sexually promiscuous and deviant since respectable women would never demean themselves by speaking in public. And yet, these women persisted, making their voices heard.

African American women exercised this same courage to bypass the patriarchal systems in the black community. The black church stood as the most powerful institution in the community and was the locus from which education and empowerment were promoted. But leadership in the black church was the domain of men, and the black church's male leaders sought to dictate the agenda. While notable African American club women of the early twentieth century were active in their churches, they sought less-restrictive platforms to extend their reach. They wanted to use their influence to determine necessary courses of action based on their experiences.

Similarly, African American women did not submit to the matriarchal systems of the white women's club movement. The white women's club movement inspired the black women's club movement, but the white clubs functioned paternalistically where matters of race were concerned. White women were often patronizing of black women, believing them to be incapable of independent leadership. African American women rejected such beliefs, demonstrating the creative ability to develop solutions, having reflected critically on communal needs. They were moved to engage collectively, and in that way, used their resources and God-given abilities to advance others.

Thus, African American women made space for their voices in leadership by overcoming oppressive systems. But that did not mean that they wanted to go it alone. Notably, African American women did not seek to exclude men or other women from the table. Instead, as the historical narrative affirms, African American women led by pooling their resources and efforts. In doing so, they promoted a shared leadership model where both men and women had a say, which is a womanist trait. Strategically, they recognized that there was strength in numbers and tacitly acknowledged that they did not have all the answers. Leveraging the power of organizing, African American women sought to bring together like-minded people who wanted to serve and improve conditions while retaining a seat at the table. It is a leadership strategy that persists with African American women to this day—welcoming everyone to the table to engage and discuss. Ironically, it was as others insisted on leading and muting the voices of African American women that they were moved to create their own organizations. But even then, African American women continued to make space for others to come alongside so that all could benefit from the positive results of collaboration.

Additionally, African American women retained a singular focus in their educational leadership efforts. They recognized the need to reach "the lowly" as an overwhelming motivator for educational advancement. Granted, the idea of reaching "the lowly" as expressed in the writings and speeches of the early club movement days sounds elitist and raises challenging contentions. Nevertheless, that desire to bridge the gap by reaching and improving those who were socially and economically disenfranchised was laudable even if not fully altruistic. As a defense against the prejudice leveled against them because of the color of their skin, educated African American women recognized the need to lift all black people. This was what led women to serve in hands-on capacities. This strategy of lifting others while climbing continues to motivate African American women's public service organizations today. By extending service to those without means and lacking opportunity, conditions are improved not only for the women touched but also those who serve and the broader community.

Learning Leadership: The Focus on Others, the Risk for Self

Such educational motivations translate to a way of leading that continues to animate the leadership style of African American women. Leadership for African American women from an educational perspective is that it is not about the one; it is about the many. I still meet too many leaders who, while advocating for others, are busy paving a path for themselves. I also meet leaders who expect their academic attainment to make them the central focus of discussions. Most African American women have not had the luxury of such personal focus. The stakes were often too high to be concerned only about self. But more importantly, self-promotion was contrary to how women were taught in the home. As a preschool child, I learned to read in part because my older female cousin would come home from school and teach me what she had learned. Such socialization of African American girls begins early. What my cousin learned, I learned, and we both benefited from it.

A related point is that womanist leadership is about the team. Again, the women's clubs are the example. The idea of a national organization resulted from the realization that an umbrella organization could help to coordinate and sharpen the impact of the work of diffused groups. The whole, being greater than the sum of its parts, was the focus. And as the team succeeded, the mission would be accomplished. Moreover, there were efforts implemented to ensure the team rose together. The NACW implemented a biennial meeting schedule in which the individual clubs would meet and hear of the innovative work taking place throughout the country. These "best practices," as we would call them today, were shared so that the individual clubs could function at the same level of excellence and efficacy as was seen in the most innovative clubs.

Additionally, educational experiences demonstrate that efforts must work collaboratively and inclusively with people to strengthen the quality of the work and the entire team. It is what leaders will frequently tell missionaries from earnest churches who want to add value: you do mission with people and not for people. The idea is to come alongside so you can hear the needs in context, understand the situation from the perspective of the people, and then work collaboratively to identify a solution. In general women have understood the need to function in this way, recognizing the hubris involved in believing someone external to the community knows the best solutions for those directly affected. Thus, womanist leadership emphasizes the need to engage and interact widely to increase learning and position the group for positive impact. African American women have learned this strategy well, recognizing that varied voices bring the best solutions.

But for all the enabling power of education and academic achievement, African American women have also recognized the challenges of pursuing such education. I remember the challenges of high school, being ostracized by African American students because of my academic strivings. I was accused of "acting white" because I earned good grades and pursued academic distinction. For instance, I was teased for attending summer school classes in history, not because I had failed in the previous term, but because I wanted to get ahead for the next year. These kinds of pressures can cause students to underperform, and some research suggests that "Black children with low levels of racial identity are less likely to achieve in school."[27] Because of such attitudes, I found high school to be an isolating experience since I did not fit in with most of my black peers.

In post-secondary education, African American women continue to suffer the obstacles seen in broader society where issues of gender and race serve as handicaps. Although the number of African American women in higher education continues to increase to the extent that some have declared African American women the most educated group in the United States, those numbers do not translate into socioeconomic status. African American women continue to struggle for positions that pay equitably with whites or black males. On average, a college education afforded white women a 4.4 percent increase in wages, but African American female college graduates' earnings were 3.2 percent lower than those of white female counterparts.[28]

And reminiscent of the challenges that confronted Mary Church Terrell in the 1880s, African American women struggle with the challenge of having their academic achievements affect their perceived marriageability. Mary Church's friends feared her educational achievements and multilinguistic abilities would condemn her to a life as a single woman. While 56 percent of white women in 2018 have never been married, 70 percent of African American women have never been married.[29] If they do marry, their mate is less likely to have achieved the same level of education. This reality raises the same domestic issues that have plagued African American families since emancipation. The promise of education is greater access to vocational opportunities, increased wages, and higher professional status. Yet this promise may come at the risk of strained relations between African American women and would-be mates.

As an African American woman, I have found that my education affects the ways I am perceived and received. Female colleagues have expressed the same issues. For example, several tell me some men regard them as intimidating. In these instances, women are treated as unapproachable, which makes social engagement difficult and may explain in part why African American women are less likely to marry. Conversely, I have had the experience where my credentials are ignored, where the prejudices of race and gender seem to eclipse credentialing such that my input is discounted. I find this especially true in male-dominated environments where it can be difficult for women to be heard or make contributions. Female colleagues in similar situations have complained their comments are ignored until a male colleague makes the same suggestion, which is then received, usually with much fanfare.[30]

The result of such marginalizing responses is that African American women respond at times in justifying ways. One colleague has become reticent in sharing her expertise, quoting other experts when making presentations for fear that her opinions would not be received as relevant. This response is born of a concern that what a woman (especially a black woman) says is insufficient. We fear that our opinions gain validity only when they are corroborated. For this colleague, it was also limiting because she constantly felt the need to reference other scholars in academic environments. Ultimately a male colleague challenged her to break the propensity to rely on external expertise before positing positions. Only then could she share her opinion without preamble, having been empowered to allow her voice to come forward.

But more often, African American women respond to these risks of perception by hiding parts of themselves as a defense mechanism. This act of hiding is referred to as the theory of dissemblance. Darlene Clark Hine writes that "as a rule," black women have "developed and adhered to a cult of secrecy, a culture of dissemblance, to protect the sanctity of inner aspects of their lives."[31] This suggests that black women refrain from making their private emotions the province of public fodder. It has been an issue of safety. African American women have historically operated in tenuous environments where disclosing their true feelings was unsafe. And whether functioning as the enslaved servant, a domestic, a factory worker, or a professional who was aware of her inequitable employment situation, these environments made it necessary for African American women to use dissemblance. Specifically, they became adept at masking their true feeling while projecting a persona of openness and transparency. "Only with secrecy, thus achieving a self-imposed invisibility, could ordinary black women accrue the psychic space and harness the resources needed to hold their own in the often one-sided and mismatched resistance struggle."[32]

While I may not have had words to explain this theory, it is a strategy I have used and watched other African American women use often in my life. Through this practice, I have learned tactics that have helped me to lead more effectively. Specifically, I have learned to be an observer. I am often discounted because of my race or gender; therefore, few people object to my silence. So, using silence to my advantage, I will often observe a meeting without verbal participation. As an observer, I engage in deep listening and watching, through which I amass information, read people, and recognize various personalities. This knowledge makes it possible to discern the best influencing strategies and employ them subtly to move a situation forward. By recognizing the dynamics of group situations, African American women have learned how to function with shrewdness, to disarm those who would be intimidated or threatened, to build up those who are disenfranchised, and to hold their thoughts to themselves, allowing people to see only what was necessary.

This chapter opened with the tongue-in-cheek remark, "Pardon my blackness, I didn't mean to shine." When collegiate classmates of my parents' era used the expression, they were offering words of encouragement to promote academic accomplishment, knowing there were those who did not recognize their aptitude. As I consider the phrase now, it seems the meaning has not changed. At the core remains an inner pride for achievement, and it matters little whether that knowledge came from home training or an academic degree. It is an inner pride that is derived at having subverted the stereotype of low expectations. It is an assertion of accomplishment even in the face of a dominant culture that doubted and discounted ability based on race. It is the recognition of a God-given ability that says I can let my light shine before men and women that all would see that light and give glory to God.

In 1930, Anna Julia Cooper, a prolific educator and scholar, delivered a speech in Buffalo, New York, asserting, "The truly powerful Negro woman has not yet arrived. But . . . someday this old world is going to reel and rock like a drunken man and the Negro woman is destined to lead women of other races into a fuller and freer atmosphere of love and of the things that are beautiful . . . and helpful in our desire to solve the great question [of race]."[33] I believe the truly powerful African American women whom Cooper sought have arrived. They have been women like her, the club women, and educators identified in this chapter. But they are also the women who continue to promote education and knowledge for themselves, their families, and their communities. As African American women have allowed their light to shine unapologetically, they illumine the path for others. They do this by coming together with an expanded view of education, from home life to advanced academic attainment, embodying a culture of uplift that was inclusive of all, functioning in nonconforming ways as intellectuals in the public square while overcoming challenges rooted in discrimination and marginalization. Pardon their blackness, they meant to shine.

Lessons in Womanist Leadership

■ Education is key. Education is an expansive concept that includes all aspects of knowledge, and we are well-served when we enable the need to learn regardless of the level.

■ Inclusivity is a must. As leaders, we must be inclusive of others, understanding that as we learn from those we are trying to serve, we are better able to serve. Moreover, leaders must be willing to listen and learn, taking the time to observe, discern, and use that knowledge to determine how best to move forward.

■ No one rises above. Our education does not make us better than others. We all run the risk of being judged by the lowest common denominator. Instead, we lift as we climb.

■ The expense of self. Promoting others can come with the risk of self. Yet, as leaders we can seek self-preserving strategies so that as we continue to lead, others may benefit from our efforts.

Notes

1. William Tullett, "Grease and Sweat: Race and Smell in Eighteenth-Century English Culture," *Cultural and Social History* 13, no. 3 (2016): 307–22; see 310.

2. Andrew S. Curran, *The Anatomy of Blackness: Science and Slavery in an Age of Enlightenment* (Baltimore: John Hopkins University Press, 2011), 158.

3. Tullett, 312.

4. Ayana D. Bird and Lori L. Tharps, *Hair Story: Untangling the Roots of Black Hair in America* (New York: St. Martin's Press, 2001), 17.

5. Tullett, 313.

6. Nikki Tang, Candrice Heath, and Nanette B. Silverberg, "Developmental Biology of Black Skin, Hair, and Nails," *Pediatric Skin of Color* (New York: Springer Science + Business Media, 2015), 16.

7. Britney C. Cooper, *Beyond Respectability: The Intellectual Thought of Race Women* (Champaign: University of Illinois Press, 2017), 11, quoting Pauline Hopkins (1902).

8. Curran, 118.

9. Ibid., 146.

10. Cooper, 18.

11. Paula Giddings, *When and Where I Enter: The Impact of Black Women on Race and Sex in America* (New York: HarperCollins, 1984), 49.

12. Cooper, 70.

13. Giddings, 109.

14. Elizabeth Lindsay Davis, *Lifting As They Climb* (New York: G. K. Hall & Co, 1996), 164.

15. Sieglinde Lemke, Introduction, in Elizabeth Lindsay Davis, *Lifting As They Climb* (New York: G. K. Hall & Co, 1996), xx.

16. Giddings, 97.

17. Lucy Craft Laney, "The Burden of the Educated Colored Woman" (1899), http://www.blackpast.org/1899-lucy-craft-laney-burden-educated-colored-woman, accessed July 13, 2018.

18. Giddings, 102.

19. Cheryl Townsend Gilkes, *If It Wasn't for the Women—: Black Women's Experience and Womanist Culture in Church and Community* (Maryknoll, NY: Orbis Books, 2001), 46.

20. Giddings, 245.

21. "Black Women Students Far Outnumber Black Men at Nation's Highest-Ranking Universities," *Journal of Blacks in Higher Education*, March 7, 2019, http://www.jbhe.com/news_views/51_gendergap_universities.html, accessed July 18, 2018.

22. Giddings, 101.

23. Audrey Thomas McCluskey, *A Forgotten Sisterhood: Pioneering Black Women Educators and Activists in the Jim Crow South* (Lanham, MD: Rowman & Littlefield, 2014), 15.

24. Giddings, 101.

25. "Black Women Students Far Outnumber Black Men at Nation's Highest-Ranking Universities."

26. Freeman A. Hrabowski III, Kenneth I. Maton, Monica L. Greene, and Geoffrey L. Greif, *Overcoming the Odds: Raising Academically Successful African American Young Women* (New York: Oxford University Press, 2002), 60.

27. Ivory A. Toldson and Delila Owens, "Acting Black": What Black Kids Think About Being Smart and Other School-related Experiences," *The Journal of Negro Education* 79, no. 2 (Spring 2010): 91–96; see 91.

28. Eboni M. Zamani, "African American Women in Higher Education," *New Directions for Student Services* 2003, issue 104, 9.

29. United States Census Bureau, Table MS-1, "Marital Status of the Population 15 Years Old and Over, by Sex, Race, and Hispanic Origin, 1950 to Present," https://www.census.gov/data/tables/time-series/demo/families/marital.html, accessed August 22, 2019.

30. This is an example of a microaggression, which is a term coined by psychiatrist and Harvard University professor Chester M. Pierce to describe insults or dismissals directed toward minorities. In this instance, an idea is ignored when offered by someone in the minority but embraced when offered by someone in the majority.

31. Darlene Clark Hine, "Rape and the Inner Lives of Black Women in the Middle West," *Signs* 14, no. 4 (Summer 1989), Common Grounds and Crossroads: Race, Ethnicity, and Class in Women's Lives, 915.

32. Ibid.

33. McCluskey, 78.

CHAPTER 5

All God's Children Got Shoes

"I got shoes, you got shoes, all God's children got shoes, my Lord . . ." To have shoes during times of enslavement was a luxury. Monies were not afforded for shoes. People were allocated an allowance for a set of work clothes and perhaps a second outfit that was worn on Sundays. Given such meager provisions, to be without shoes or perhaps given cast-off, ill-fitting shoes was a marker of enslavement. And understanding this condemning marker, we can appreciate the actions of the prodigal son's father, as recorded in Luke 15:22. When the father recognized his returning son in the distance, the father instructed his slaves to bring a robe, ring, and sandals for his son. The son was robed, which was a symbol of restoration. It did not matter what the son had done; he had been forgiven by his father. The son was given a ring to signify that he was empowered to be a representative of his father. And he was given shoes for his feet, meaning that he was not a slave but was a beloved son. To have shoes was a designation of status. But, as seen with the prodigal son, it was also a sign of adoption and inclusion. As such, the unknown author of this African American religious folk song envisioned a day when all of God's children would have shoes, symbolizing their recognition and inclusion as the sons and daughters of God.

This is an image of justice: an image in which God's children would have all that was needed but not provided as the result of enslavement. Justice was a common theme in spiritual music. The songs composed by enslaved Africans or their descendants envisioned fairness, equity, provision, and grace made available to all. These tenets are what the enslaved came to recognize in Christianity, but the unjust discrepancies between Christian doctrine and Christian practice slowed its adoption by enslaved Africans. Notably, adoption was also affected by the importation of new captives from western and central Africa, whose arrival strengthened the use of religious practices that migrated from their homeland.[1] Yet had religious practice more consistently followed doctrine, Christianity would have been more readily embraced. The African belief system emphasizes love of humanity, commitment to justice, and the ultimate rule of divine will,[2] which is consistent with Christianity. However, given the hypocrisy of a religion whose practice did not cohere with doctrine, when the songwriter wrote, "Everybody talkin' 'bout heaven ain't going there," the meaning was clear: those who claimed to be Christian but refused to extend justice to all would be excluded from heaven in the final judgment. Slave masters and those who upheld the institution of slavery would come to experience separation from God for all eternity. Conversely, the oppressed would enjoy freedom, whether that freedom was as an escapee in the present or as a citizen in God's eternal community in the afterlife. To realize such justice was the cause of celebration in song. Slave masters missed the meaning because the words were shrouded by upbeat tunes, jubilant dancing, and praise. But the good news was unmasked. Not only would all of God's children have shoes, but also the unjust would receive divine punishment.

For African American women, however, this song engenders additional sentiments. First, to suggest that we can celebrate a time when all have what they need speaks of communal equity. If I have shoes, then it follows that you must have shoes as well. There would be no dichotomy of those who have versus those who do not have. Reminiscent of the first-century church as recorded in Acts 2:44-45, "All who believed were together and had all things in common; they would sell their possessions and goods and distribute the proceeds to all, as any had need." The goal was an inclusive community where there was provision for everyone.

Second, to say everyone has shoes was to promote the importance of a just stance, where advocacy helped to promote equity. The song's author was emboldened to envision a time when everyone would have their needs met, and when they would be counted among the righteous of God through their inclusion. In sharing that vision, others, as they sang and embraced the words, could also dream of that just life for themselves and for their families. Thus, the spark of one becomes a catalyzing spark for community. The willingness of one to assert a just stance moves others as well, promoting a vision of equity for all.

Arguably such a just stance is the most important aspect of the term "womanist," as defined by Alice Walker. In womanist practice, justice is a central construct, manifested by an insistence that a womanist is committed to survival and wholeness of an entire people, male and female.[3] A focus on the whole requires the coming together of people in unity and in community, and the assurance of communal flourishing, which is achieved when needs were satisfied. Thus, a womanist is not interested in separating from men or realizing an identity that is disconnected from men. Survival for African American people has required men and women to unify. People's needs and wants are met through community, which requires the full partnership of women and men in creation with God, modeling and embodying inclusivity enveloped by justice.[4]

The mechanics of a communal model are embedded in African culture, with women playing a significant role in community. The African culture that migrated to the United States with enslaved Africans featured shared responsibilities between men and women, with certain communal responsibilities being led by women. Specifically, the cultural mores and value systems of tribes and communities were passed through the female members of society.[5] Women ensured the beliefs and values were embedded in communal practices. As women shared and lived a way of being that fostered a culture of communal care, these practices were appropriated and continued generationally. We recognize such tenets in the stories of African Americans raised in the mid twentieth century.

For example, I heard the stories of my parents who spoke of being disciplined by neighbors when they were caught misbehaving.

Because it was the community's responsibility to participate in the care of children, to be punished corporally by another adult was a frequent practice. Not only would the neighbor take it upon herself to reprimand you, but she would also notify your parents of the observed transgressions, which ensured that additional punishment was meted out once you arrived at home. For me, the community also collaborated to ensure the safe arrival at school. As the neighborhood's children walked together, women in the community served as informal monitors stationed along the way, waving at us from windows in greeting or chiding us to get moving as we made our way to school. I remember telling my mother how Miss Geneva would wave at us every day as we walked to school. I thought it was coincidence, but my mother nodded knowingly. Everyone was involved because that was what it meant to be community. In community, people are unified and together; they ensure inclusive care, advocate for what is right, and promote these beliefs, instilling them in future generations. Thus, it is impossible to talk about womanist leadership without considering the importance of community.

The African American woman's embrace of community and matters of justice is core to her being, yet the injustice of intersectionality, that simultaneous oppression of race, gender, and class, tears at communal cohesion because marginalization divides people. African American women were historically moved to advocate on behalf of their communities to promote justice. The inherent dignity and right of every individual required such stances, and it was not enough to contain efforts to the confines of the home. African American women demonstrated this in their communal involvements.

For example, the women's club movement first gained traction among white women before becoming popular with African American women. However, in comparison, the white women's clubs served a greater social function. Conversely, African American women, seeing the injustices in their communities, were not satisfied to limit themselves to the social skills, even as the desire for respectability required the mastery of such graces. Going beyond what was deemed to be a woman's role, African American women donned unfashionable stances to engage in efforts to lift a community, as noted in chapter 4. This was foundational to who they were. Faith was also a primary motivator for communal involvement. Countless narratives exist of women's church organizations and auxiliaries devoting themselves to efforts on behalf of their communities. Not limited to Bible study and community service, church women took Jesus' words to heart: "For I was hungry and you gave me food, I was thirsty and you gave me something to drink, I was a stranger and you welcomed me, I was naked and you gave me clothing, I was sick and you took care of me, I was in prison and you visited me."[6] Jesus required that we go forth to serve, and women, obeying his command, did just that. They saw a broader mission field, which extended their efforts to secular affairs. Some women's auxiliaries advocated for anti-lynching legislation, crusaded for temperance, and challenged segregation, engaging in an activist religion that urged others to act as positive agents for change in the world.[7] Others, emboldened by their activist stances and communal needs, also saw fit to seek elected office to effect the changes they promoted.

From these examples and experiences, we see an emerging system of beliefs that explains why African American women led with a focus on community. Communal engagement was embedded in the culture and motivated women to care for and insist on justice for the whole through an animating faith that required action. Moreover, that action motivated African American women to move beyond comfortable spheres of influence to community-based advocacy for civil rights and political involvement. Girded by their beliefs, many women became the unsung heroines for communal change.

This is seen particularly during the civil rights movement of the 1950s and 1960s, "which was carried largely by women."[8] Women had to lead because black men were the overwhelming targets of retribution as African Americans sought civil rights. The Equal Justice Initiative asserted that through lynching and other extrajudicial acts of violence, white men wielded their power over black men through targeted torture and death when black men were perceived as step-ping outside their relegated social roles by achieving economic suc-cess or demanding better treatment.[9] Public displays of punishment and execution served as an effective means of silencing the advocacy efforts of African American men. Men ran the risk of losing their lives by attempting to assert their rights as human beings or defend-ing their homes and families. While women were also victims of lynching and other such violent acts, they were targeted to a lesser degree. This reality positioned women to lead the movement. As so-cial scientist E. Franklin Frazier noted, "In the South, the middle-class Negro male is not only prevented from playing a masculine role, but generally, he must let Negro women assume leadership in any show of militancy."[10]

Men were also at times reticent to lead, as was the case for African American clergymen. Male clergy were sought to serve as commu-nity organizing and civil rights leaders because of the power and cen-trality of the black church, yet the black church was slow to respond. Perhaps it was concern over retribution toward the church or male leader, or belief that political involvement was not the domain of the church, but the result was a hesitant silence. Even Martin Luther King Jr. recognized that the national black denominations never mus-tered their full resources to the struggle, and the National Baptist Convention refused to be identified with him.[11] The level of ambiva-lence was high in the church with many wanting to exercise caution over involvement. In response, the Nation of Islam was particularly critical of the black church, noting that "the black Christian preacher is the white man's most effective tool for keeping the so-called Ne-groes pacified and controlled."[12]

In response, women stepped forward to lead but did so from back-ground positions because the desire to promote an emerging great man as leader persisted. To that point, Martin Luther King Jr. em-phasized the civil rights movement made him rather than he, as the charismatic leader, making the movement.[13] He was a twenty-six-year-old pastor at the time of the 1956 Montgomery bus boycott.

New to Montgomery, Alabama, King had little time to distinguish himself in the community. But seeking a great man, community leaders pushed King into the spotlight. Women did not seek such spotlights but instead assumed background tasks. For example, women circulated flyers calling for a bus boycott to coincide with the court date upon which Rosa Parks was tried for refusing to give up her bus seat to a white man. It was after this successful women-led boycott that the Montgomery Improvement Association was formed and King named its president.

African American women were the ones who sparked a countercultural leadership movement, using their agency to galvanize others and create space for community response rather than awaiting the great individual leader or leadership from the church.

Ella Baker: Civil Rights Movement Leader and Champion

Ella Baker embodied such characteristics, and from her early upbringing, we recognize the inherent womanist leadership qualities that motivated her. Ella Baker was born in 1903 in Norfolk, Virginia, and she "grew up in a female-centered household, surrounded by a community of Christian women actively engaged in uplifting their families and communities."[14] Although her grandparents were enslaved, her parents were able to attend secondary school, thus instilling a focus on education. Her maternal grandfather was a noted Baptist pastor, and her mother played an active role in the Baptist church, which provided a foundation of faith for Baker. Being raised in the south by parents who were able to distinguish themselves through education, Baker was encouraged to be exceptional, constantly reminded that humility and service to others were Christian virtues she was required to uphold. Baker's family believed those who enjoyed academic opportunities, middle-class status, and relative privilege had a fundamental obligation to work for the improvement of their race and, especially, to improve the conditions of the many women and children who were denied such advantages.[15]

These beliefs propelled Ella Baker's community service work. She drew on a foundation of faith, employed the resources of her education, and, recognizing the needs of others, directed her efforts toward community. After graduating from Shaw University, Baker moved to New York as part of the great migration of African Americans who left the south seeking better opportunities in the north. She settled in Harlem, which was a hotbed of political activity following the Harlem Renaissance of the 1920s. Believing that her college education would afford her greater employment opportunities, Baker was shocked to find that she was even turned down for the low-paying job of addressing envelopes because there were so many applicants.[16] But her unemployment created a sense of solidarity with the working poor. In fact, she was so troubled by the impact of the 1929 stock market crash on African Americans in Harlem that she was moved to collaborate with friends to form the Young Negroes' Cooperative League (YNCL), an organization that helped African American consumers learn the benefits of cooperative buying power, enabling them to take control of their own economic outcomes.[17]

In her efforts, Baker modeled a collaborative and group-centered form of leadership in that she did not seek to establish or lead the organization independently. Rather, she promoted communal, collective agency utilizing a bottom-up approach that sought to empower those who had been disenfranchised. Furthermore, the charter of the organization "pledged itself to the full inclusion and equal participation of women."[18] While such a leadership approach may have been regarded as unique, it harkened to the community of women Baker saw operating in her formative years. This grassroots model taught her that people empowered could do for themselves.

Baker also modeled the characteristic of doing what needed to be done without regard to fanfare or attention. With Martin Luther King Jr. and his confidants, the heralded activists Bayard Rustin and Stanley Levinson, she collaborated to form the Southern Christian Leadership Conference (SCLC) in January 1957. However, from the outset, the organization reinforced the belief in the "great man" leader, naming

King as the head of the organization with the related expectation that male clergy would step forward to lead civil rights efforts in their communities. Ella Baker was tapped to run its office and do the groundwork required to develop the organization.

While there was a desire to have a great man at the top, someone needed to do the work, and Baker was willing to supply the sweat equity necessary to form a fledging organization. She garnered support for the organization and created a network through which it could operate. Her initial intent was to work for SCLC "for six weeks, but its lack of funds made it difficult to find a replacement who had the skills and willingness to perform the unglamorous development spadework so sorely needed."[19] In other words, the organization needed a skilled leader but had no monies for compensation. Indicative of the ways of African American women leaders, Baker remained with the organization, even given insufficient remuneration, and effectively became the first executive director of SCLC. Yet what may have been viewed as a senior-level, strategic role was menially intensive. When Baker relocated to Atlanta from New York to assume her role, the organization's headquarters was nonexistent. No one had made provisions for space. The organization had a designated leader and other clergy to serve as the face of the organization, but there was no office or phone for use. As Baker herself said, in those early days, she functioned "out of a telephone booth and [her] pocketbook."[20] Nevertheless, because of her efforts, SCLC became an operational entity.

Even with these demonstrated abilities, Baker was never afforded the official title of executive director. King considered Baker only an "acting" or interim director, seeming to be against her permanent appointment because she was neither male nor clergy.[21] These sexist biases notwithstanding, Baker served in this role for two and a half years. But tensions, which were rooted in sexist perspectives, mounted. King held a hierarchical view of leadership, noting, "Leadership never ascends from the pew to the pulpit, but . . . descends from the pulpit to the pew."[22] This view was opposite to that of Baker. She believed that the oppressed did not need a messiah to deliver them; "all they needed was themselves, one another, and the will to persevere."[23] Never seeking the limelight but wanting to empower the people, Baker exhibited her belief that everyone could be a leader, and she was a lightning rod for such a way of leading.

In 1960, students from North Carolina Agriculture & Technical College in Greensboro, North Carolina, staged a sit-in protesting segregation at a local store. Baker saw this as an opportunity to galvanize student activism and leadership. Leveraging resources from SCLC and utilizing facilities at her alma mater, Shaw University, Baker convened more than three hundred students for what would become the Student Nonviolent Coordinating Conference.[24] Baker was fifty-seven years old at the time, but she did not attempt to foist her experience onto the students. She encouraged them to start their own organization, wanting them to think for themselves and realize the solutions that resulted from their inner and collective wisdom. Although she did not attempt to lead the SCLC from a hierarchical perspective, she was credited for imparting guiding principles that helped students find their way in their efforts. Specifically, she encouraged them to:

1. Identify and begin with the needs of the people with whom one is working;

2. Recognize the value of innovation that comes from different viewpoints;

3. Recognize the value of small groups;

4. Establish relationships between the organizer and the people with whom one is working, especially across race, class, and gender boundaries;

5. Develop local leadership;

6. Resist hierarchical, traditional leadership that is competitive, authoritarian, and charismatic;

7. Recognize the plodding, unglamorous, every day, unrewarded nature of organizing;

8. Appreciate the strength and value of Southern folk culture.[25]

Baker's guiding principles were a catalyst for social change and grass-roots leadership, but they were also the culmination of life stories, experiences, and markers that I believe demonstrate how African American women lead. In fact, if one sought to summarize what womanist leadership looks like in community, Baker's guiding principles would fit the bill.

Begin with the Needs of the People / The first principle that Baker's life demonstrates is that community organizing must begin with the people of the community, and women inherently understood the need to work with people where they were. Baker learned this as she co-wrote with Marvel Cooke the *New York Amsterdam News* article entitled "Bronx Slave Market," about women who waited on street corners in hopes that Bronx housewives would "buy" them for slave wages to do housework.[26] The article shared the experiences of unemployed African American women who were exploited and paid only pennies per hour to clean houses or wash windows. The article also intimated that men came to the street corners in hopes of hiring women for sexual favors. While some women did sell themselves for money, women interviewed in the article hesitated to pass judgment because times were hard. To chastise women for doing what they needed to do, even if at times that meant selling their bodies, was an ineffectual approach. Baker knew this. In advocating for the women, Baker needed to empathize with their situation from their perspective and engage in ways that spoke to their condition. Only then would progress be made. Baker used this concept to bring people together and commonly used a Socratic rhetorical process, drawing people out and posing questions to stimulate thinking, to help them identify critically and creatively their own solutions.[27]

Recognize the Value of Different Viewpoints / Second, Baker recognized that innovation resulted from different viewpoints, and in her efforts, she sought to discover such perspectives to encourage learning and unique ways to move forward. Such a strategy is rooted in standpoint theory, which recognizes the validity of everyone's standpoint and accepts that knowledge is situationally located, based on experience. The astute leader attempts to draw upon these viewpoints to gain strength from shared wisdom. In her study with African American female executives, Patricia Parker noted that African American women in executive positions employed this tactic by encouraging collaborative debate. They did this to solicit diverse viewpoints, which I would add is the impetus for innovation. Collaborative debate is a method of dialectic inquiry that invites people with opposing opinions to provide input via one-to-one arguments to expose points of agreement and refutation and ultimately reach a collaboratively determined decision.[28] By engaging people with varying opinions, the best ideas can rise to the fore and the collaborating group realizes ownership of those ideas together.

Recognize the Value of Small Groups / A third principle is that the strategy of collaborative debate is arguably more efficient when employed in small groups. Small groups often encourage participation from those who are otherwise marginalized or see themselves as culturally powerless. I participated in a multicultural gathering in which participants were grouped for discussion with people of their own ethnicity and culture. I noted that in the first round of the exercise, the conversations were lively with most participants engaged in discussion because people were paired with people who were culturally and ethnically like them. In the second round, participants were paired with people of the same and different ethnicities and cultures. Discussions continued, but fewer people were engaged in conversation. By the third round, the small groups were well-mixed, leaving many minorities as the only member of their culture or ethnicity in the group. My third-round group included a Latina and Haitian woman and two white men. The men deferentially invited the women to speak first, but the Latina and Haitian women, who were visibly uncomfortable with the invitation to share, declined. In response, I watched the white men nonverbally communicate a message that seemed to say, "Well, we tried," after which they proceeded to monopolize the conversation.

I was not surprised. When people of color come together in a group setting, they expect an authoritative leader to take the lead and tell them what should happen.[29] This response is based on the dynamics of power, how it is perceived, and the effects of cultural orientation. People who have not traditionally had power will not automatically assume power because it is offered. The women in my group were unprepared for and uncomfortable with assuming the power to put forth their opinions. The white men, conversely, were very comfortable with seizing power. In fact, their level of comfort in taking control of the conversation made their invitation to the women to speak appear paternalistic. When the women deferred, the men that happily took charge of the discussion. Thus, my experience demonstrates that the use of small groups does not guarantee participation, but it does uncover power dynamic inequities based on culture and ethnicity. In this instance, although the women were comfortable remaining silent, they were not able to maintain the same level of anonymity possible in a larger group setting because all were aware they were not contributing in the small-group context. To encourage participation, Eric Law created mutual invitation with multicultural groups.[30] In this process, the speaker has the privilege of inviting another person to share, and the invitee has the option of sharing or passing to another speaker. The process has as a goal to decentralize power in a group by ensuring that all have had equal opportunities to share through invitation. The combination of a small-group discussion format with mutual invitation ensures all are heard and made part of the conversation.

Establish Relationships across Boundaries / Fourth, Baker recognized the need to establish relationships between the organizer and the people with whom she was working, especially across race, class, and gender boundaries. I contend that her cross-boundary work was influenced by her experiences with intersectionality. The interdependent effects of multiple oppressions make it impossible to confront race, gender, or class in isolation. Therefore, bringing people together across divides provided a multidimensional strategy to address oppressions collectively. In addition, by encouraging people to establish relationships, Baker was fostering community, which enables participants to realize a sense of belonging and mutual dependence. Through greater dependence and belonging, trust can flourish. Collectively, when these attributes are present, people are more likely to seek points of agreement, engage in respectful deliberations, and emerge with increased self-esteem and well-being. Working across intersectional boundaries also dismantles power imbalances because relationships make it possible for people to cooperate rather than combat.

Develop Local Leaders / Baker's views on leadership, that leadership be shared and that leaders be locally identified, serve as a fifth principle and were shaped in her community organizing work. She recognized the resultant power from decisions being made, owned, and shared by the people most affected. For example, in 1956, Baker, along with Stanley Levinson and Bayard Rustin, founded the organization In Friendship, which offered financial support to activists in the deep south.[31] Her desire was to find someone who was local and support them in their efforts. Baker recognized that local people knew what their problems were. If they were given resources to develop themselves and come together, they would be most successful in identifying their own solutions. In support of her beliefs, she instituted training workshops so that people would learn the work at the grassroots level. She wanted to be an enabling resource to help people rather than do the work for them.

Resist Hierarchical, Traditional Leadership That Is Competitive, Authoritarian, and Charismatic / The sixth principle stands as a contrasting corollary to principle five. To develop local leaders meant that communities needed to resist hierarchical, traditional leadership that was competitive, authoritarian, and charismatic. Her work with the SCLC only cemented this position. Baker lamented her subservient position there, where people mistook her as a "glorified secretary" for Martin Luther King Jr.,[32] and she flippantly remarked that she was kept in the position because someone needed to run the mimeograph machine.[33] Being so disregarded, she came to hold antipathy for hierarchical models of leadership that valued authoritarian and charismatic characteristics. These charismatic leaders infrequently rolled up their sleeves to do the work. They instead gloried in the opportunity to offer speeches, rarely engaging those on the ground. And seeing so many examples of black clergy who operated in dictatorial fashions or who seemingly abused their power, she came to conclude, "That's a group of people I can do without."[34] It was the local leaders, properly engaged and trained, who would carry the momentum and accomplish the tasks at hand.

Recognize the Plodding Nature of Organizing / The seventh principle was the need to recognize the unglamorous work of organizing. Baker knew firsthand the types of preparation needed before and after advocacy events. SCLC leaders arrived at designated locations to speak, but organizing leadership was needed prior to the event and afterward to ensure the momentum generated could continue. We still glory over the success of the March on Washington in August 1963. But it was Ella Baker who decided where to rally, pulled the permits to make the march possible, prepared the bail for potential arrests, and called the media to notify them of the event.[35] Such administrative detail is so seemingly trivial that none would think to herald it. But someone had to do the work. African American women were well-acquainted with the essential but unglamorous background work because so often this was the work relegated to women. But Baker recognized that without this work being done, the events that would be celebrated as momentous decades later could not have happened.

Appreciate the Strength of Southern Folk Culture / The final principle has significant resonance for womanist leadership because a prime method for understanding culture is through story. Baker remembered hearing the stories of her maternal grandmother, Elizabeth "Bet" Ross, who often recounted for her the experiences and challenges of enslavement. In one example, Bet, the child of her master and enslaved mother, refused to marry the man her owners designated for her, suffering whipping and field labor instead, and ultimately choosing her own husband. Bet resisted "the will of her slave mistress and master to define her own humanity," a story she took great pride in retelling to her grandchildren.[36] The narrative instilled the value of personal and political resistance and that Baker descended from a long line of militant fighters.[37] As she gleaned the strength of her grandmother's story, Baker was able to utilize that story in her life to sustain her. More importantly, having been girded with this countercultural militancy, she was unapologetic in carving out new spaces for her witness. These are the strengths and characteristics that students saw in her when they named her "'Fundi,' the Swahili title of honor for that person who is valued for her or his expertise within the community and who passes on what has been learned to the next generation through example and instruction."[38]

Inspiration for Advocacy

Baker's story, the principles that she imparted, and her way of being demonstrate the inspiration for advocacy so commonly seen in the lives of African American heroines. They drew upon a knowledge base: a knowledge rooted in faith, education, or convictions of what was right, which was an exercise of agency, and they demonstrated and trusted in their own capacity to make meaning in their context. Then comparing what they believed to be true with inconsistencies observed in their environment, they were emboldened to act. The actions were varied, possibly drawing on diverse strategies, and at times countercultural, but through engagement their efforts unmasked the injustices of the dominant system.

One example of this effort to unmask systems of injustice was seen in an organization that was important to Baker when she moved to Harlem: the Young Women's Christian Association (YWCA). The

New York City YWCA, which served African American women in the city, sought affiliated status with the Fifteenth Street YWCA, which served white women. However, when the Fifteenth Street executive committee's approval was predicated on the condition that they have no fiscal responsibility for the New York City branch but retain constitutional connectivity, which ensured subordinated status, they were shocked to learn the African American women rejected their stated terms.[39] The conditions established by the Fifteenth Street YWCA executive board demonstrated racist attitudes. They did not believe the African American founders of the New York City YWCA had "the capacity—material, moral, or intellectual—to administer such an institution successfully."[40] As a result, they did not want to be financially responsible for the New York YWCA but did want to ensure a controlling relationship to dictate operations.

The African American women could have acquiesced to the conditions. The relationship, even in its preconditioned state, would have enabled them to accomplish their goals. Specifically, the YWCA was established to foster "religious awakening in young, self-supporting Protestant woman as a supplement to their church attendance,"[41] and African American women desired this same agency for young women in their community. Moreover, the YWCA movement represented for women an opportunity to provide a targeted focus to their religious convictions. However, the African American women understood that to acquiesce was to participate in the unjust dominant structure that relegated African Americans to a second-class status. Therefore, they rejected the conditions. Their refusal demonstrated agency, as the women chose not to cooperate with a system that sought to degrade. Additionally, their refusal demonstrated advocacy. They advocated for themselves in their abilities to lead and advocated for future generations who would come to understand their stance.

These kinds of stances were common for African American women. These women were nurtured in community and benefited from communal support. Therefore, it logically followed that women would devote their efforts to the communal context, leveraging their individual and collective resources, and do what was needed for the betterment of their communities. It was a cooperative response that observed a mutual responsibility for one another. This was the example of civil rights leader Dorothy Height, who said her mother taught her the importance of being cooperative rather than competitive based on her responsibility to others.[42] She took this responsibility to heart even as she continued her studies. Height hoped to gain an academic scholarship by entering an essay contest, for which she studied the language of the Thirteenth, Fourteenth, and Fifteenth Amendments. In her studies, Height recognized "the gaps between what the Constitution promised and what people of color experienced every day," and she was moved to action because she saw it as her responsibility.[43] Height dedicated her life to advocacy, attempting to ensure the enforcement of what were called the Reconstruction Amendments. Height's example is like Baker's: she drew upon life lessons reinforced by her mother; she used her academic abilities to understand the context; she trusted her sense of justice that identified the inconsistencies between theory and practice; and she acted, devoting her life to community service for others.

Having met Dr. Height, I do not believe that she would have necessarily declared herself to be a womanist. She was simply doing what she believed to be right. In a session I hosted for Delta Sigma Theta sorority on running for office, Dr. Height, a past president of the organization, made extemporaneous comments about leadership and team development. She dismissed the idea of competition, promoting the need to bring the best people together, divergent opinions notwithstanding. Height recognized that diverse teams were positioned to realize the best ideas and make the greatest impact. Her focus on impact was far more important than recognition, as history demonstrates. Height was the only woman of the civil rights inner circle who was on the stage with King during his "I Have Dream" speech. Although she was an integral part of the planning and execution of the March on Washington, Height's name is rarely mentioned. However, her anonymity did not seem to faze her because recognition was not important. Embracing the lessons she was taught by her mother, she gave back to community. Moreover, she used her leadership influence to ensure the best and brightest came together to reach the goal, even as she minimized the importance of her efforts. This is what she did as a civil rights leader, and it is what she modeled when she offered her comments during my gathering.

Community-Focused Leadership Model

How then do these traits of African American women who have been nurtured in community, imbued with a sense of justice, motivated to advocacy, and inspired to respond on behalf of others come together to inform our leadership? The adage reminds us that charity begins at home and then spreads abroad, and in similar fashion, African American women have created a leadership developmental model that demonstrates a generationally progressive transmission from women, to their children, and into community. Authors Toni C. King and S. Alease Ferguson articulated that model, recognizing four foundational developmental stages with two additional cross-cutting characteristics to depict womanist leadership in community.

First, they suggested that at the foundation, African American women taught their children basic habitational skills, which are the habits of personal grooming, hygiene, and self-governance.[44] These are the lessons that harken to respectability, which were instilled through home training. While respectability was important, these lessons also enhanced self-esteem, providing children with a sense of place and pride, while helping them to understand relational skills, proper conduct, and appearance. In a sermon illustration, I shared with a Ghanaian congregation that my mother would lick her fingers to claim stray marks from my face to ensure that I was publicly presentable. Hating that practice as a child, I had promised myself I would never subject my children to such a ritual, but as a parent, I found I too utilized the spittle bath as needed on occasion. Every woman in the congregation connected with my illustration because all had given or received similar baths. I was particularly heartened by the resonance. The connection demonstrated a realized community from which my African American upbringing did not leave me estranged. It was truly diasporic and indicative of a basic lesson that woman of African ancestry would impart to their children.

Second, African American women foster communal affiliation as a means of promoting skills development. Children need to be able to see themselves as part of a community, and one of the most efficacious ways of achieving this goal is by engaging in chores that support the community. Such development is rooted in the notion of collective work or Ujima, which is the third principle of the African American Kwanzaa celebration. By engaging in collective, cooperative work, children see their place as important in community. Additionally, age-appropriate chores help them to cultivate a work ethic and internalize cooperative behaviors so that the needs and challenges of the community become theirs as well. Children who are engaged in the work of the family through appropriate chores learn what it means to serve and how important their contributions in service can be. They also develop a sense of self-sufficiency, autonomy, and pride in learning and doing a task well.

The third leadership developmental trait that African American women transmit to their children is a work ethic that promotes continuing vocational maturity. This development stage recognizes that our responsibilities in community increase as we mature. I remember as a four-year-old asking my mother if I could wash dishes. My parents accommodated me by bringing a chair upon which I could stand so I could wash the dishes. Little did I know that this would become my lifelong chore. As I aged, it became my responsibility to wash dishes. However, over time, that chore expanded to fully cleaning the kitchen— wiping counters and cabinets, sweeping floors, and cleaning the refrigerator of food relegated to the category of science project. Through this progression, I learned mastery as my responsibilities increased. And through this mastery, I was prepared for greater efforts because I had cultivated a work ethic that was required in my adult life.

These formational leadership development skills prepare children for the fourth developmental trait, which is full citizenship in community because it fosters social independence and functional interdependence. Social independence is realized as children gain a work ethic, engendering personal pride in their individual efforts. Functional interdependence is realized as children experience cooperative engagement in community, which creates belonging. Both independence and interdependence are needed to create well-rounded communal contributors, as we see in the life stories of Ella Baker and Dorothy Height. Baker helped to look after children in the community who were being raised by a single father, while Height helped a child struggling in school so that he too would understand his lessons. Their life stories demonstrate a community of women who helped them see a place for themselves through service and responsibility, because they had tasks that they were required to carry out. Taking pride in their ability to contribute, they continued to give back to their community, demonstrating interdependence. Following the Gospel of Luke, "To whom much is given, much is required,"[45] they gave back as full citizens of the community.

Then there are the two cross-cutting characteristics that African American women provide to their children as part of leadership development: social justice consciousness and capacities for resistance. These characteristics are particularly personal to me as the mother of an African American male because I recognize the injustices of a system that unfairly conspires against him. I remember one day when my son came into the house brandishing a plastic gun borrowed from a friend saying, "This is a robbery!" My husband and I recognized that the gun was a plastic toy, and we correctly concluded that our son had borrowed it from the group of kids with whom he was playing. But we were also aware that Tamir Rice had had a plastic gun as well, and that fact did not stop police from gunning him down. My son was twelve years old at the time, just as was Tamir Rice. And in response, our family, my husband, my oldest stepson, and I, launched into a social justice consciousness lesson for our son. We wanted him to know that it was not fair, because any of his (white) friends outside could similarly brandish a gun and people would think nothing of it.

However, as an African American male, he could not do the same. While we wanted to speak into his life strategies for agency and the ability to hold to his convictions, we also knew it was imperative for us to ensure that he could successfully navigate the societal injustices for his personal safety.

However, it is this need for a social justice consciousness that also requires that African American women provide for their children capacities for resistance. Simultaneously with infusing a social justice consciousness, African American parents help their children build up an ability to resist and speak for themselves concerning oppression. My husband and I want our child to know that he is exceptional. My grandfather once saw my mother's name printed on the program for a community-wide event, and uttered with pride, "My people are somebody." In that same vein, my son is somebody. We do not want him to think of himself more highly than he ought, but at the same time, we want him to be able to stand in the face of oppression. On our refrigerator is a sign his grandmother created, saying, "I am a child of God and I can do all things through Christ who strengthens me." It serves as a daily affirmation for our son. And together these capacities do exactly what Toni C. King and S. Alease Ferguson suggest: they dismantle oppression and promote social justice in any context in which we participate.

Shoes for Everybody

"I've got shoes and you've got shoes. All God's children got shoes, my Lord." It is not a request. It is an increasingly urgent demand for justice to which African American women have dedicated themselves to ensuring that the broader community has what it needs. The demand demonstrates agency as African American women have been emboldened to speak for self and on behalf of others. It also speaks of a social justice consciousness that says, "I deserve shoes." Shoes, which are symbolic for all that is needed to prosper in society, are not the domain of the powerful. Everyone deserves shoes. And if our social justice consciousness has the audacity to demand shoes, then we must build the competencies of personal empowerment that compel people to remain firm in their insistence.

My grandfather once shared that, in his day, African American people needed to step aside from the sidewalk if a white person was passing. Knowing my father, I am certain he never stepped off a sidewalk for someone, and considering my son, he would be offended by the suggestion. My son has such a well-developed sense of self and such an intolerance for injustice that he would naturally resist any act that would attempt to diminish him or his personhood. This is the type of response womanist leadership seeks to foster in community. As we give ourselves in community, the entire community is empowered to rise and demand what they require because justice demands they deserve it.

Lessons in Womanist Leadership

■ Orient your efforts toward community. Every aspect of the African American woman's experience orients her to serving in community. Living as followers of Jesus Christ demands that we serve.

■ Expand your standpoint and advocate for all. The intersectional standpoint which is based on racial, gender, and class oppression demands that we advocate so that others are not oppressed.

■ Grow at the grassroots. A womanist way of leading in community focuses efforts at the grassroots level, empowers others, develops new leaders who are aided in finding their voices, and engages in the unglamorous background work, without concern for self-promotion.

■ Champion communal involvement with children. African American women propagate the culture of communal involvement through a leadership development method that teaches children from the earliest age what it means to be a part of community.

Notes

1. Arthur C. Jones, *Wade in the Water: The Wisdom of the Spirituals* (Maryknoll, NY: Orbis Books, 1993), 7.

2. Ibid.

3. Cheryl Townsend Gilkes, "Womanist Ways of Seeing," in *Black Theology: A*

Documentary History, vol. 2: *1980–1992*, ed. James H. Cone and Gayraud S. Wilmore (1993; Maryknoll, NY: Orbis Books, 2003), 323.

4. Ibid., 322.

5. Diana L. Hayes, *Hagar's Daughters: Womanist Ways of Being in the World* (Mahwah, NJ: Paulist Press, 1995), 18.

6. Matthew 25:35-36.

7. Barbara Ransby, *Ella Baker and the Black Freedom Movement: A Radical Democratic Vision* (Chapel Hill: University of North Carolina Press, 2003), 17.

8. Paula Giddings, *When and Where I Enter: The Impact of Black Women on Race and Sex in America* (1984; New York: Harper Collins, 2006), 259; the quote is from Ella Baker.

9. Equal Justice Initiative, "Lynching in America: Confronting the Legacy of Racial Terror," https://web.archive.org/web/20180510151602/https://lynchinginamerica.eji.org/report/, accessed February 7, 2019.

10. Giddings, 258.

11. Gayraud S. Wilmore, *Black Religion and Black Radicalism: An Interpretation of the Religious History of Afro-American People* (Maryknoll, NY: Orbis Books, 1983), 179.

12. Ibid., 173.

13. Albert J. Raboteau, *American Prophets: Seven Religious Radicals and Their Struggle for Social and Political Justice* (Princeton, NJ: Princeton University Press, 2016), 141.

14. Ransby, 15.

15. Ibid.

16. Ibid., 67, 68.

17. Mittie K. Carey, "The Parallel Rhetorics of Ella Baker," *Southern Communication Journal* 79, no. 1 (January–March 2014), 30.

18. Ransby, 83.

19. Giddings, 269.

20. Ransby, 181.

21. Marilyn Bordwell DeLaure, "Planting Seeds of Change: Ella Baker's Radical Rhetoric," *Women's Studies in Communication* 31, no. 1 (Spring 2018): 1–28; see 1, 11.

22. Adam Fairclough, *Martin Luther King Jr.* (Athens: University of Georgia Press, 1995), 19.

23. Ransby, 188.

24. Aprele Elliott, "Ella Baker: Free Agent of Change," *Journal of Black Studies* 26, no. 5 (May 1996), Special Issue: The Voices of African American Women in the Civil Rights Movement, 600.

25. Susan M. Glisson, "'Neither Bedecked Nor Bebosomed': Lucy Randolph Mason, Ella Baker, and Women's Leadership and Organizing in the Struggle for Freedom," PhD dissertation, the College of William and Mary in Virginia, UMI 2001, 164–65.

26. Marvel Cooke, "Slavery . . . 1939 Style," *New York Amsterdam News* (1938–1941); May 27, 1939, 17.

27. Elliott, 600.

28. Patricia S. Parker, *Race, Gender and Leadership: Re-Envisioning Organizational Leadership from the Perspectives of African American Women Executives* (2005; New York: Psychology Press, 2015), 69.

29. Eric H. F. Law, *The Wolf Shall Dwell with the Lamb: A Spirituality for Leadership in a Multicultural Community* (St. Louis, MO: Chalice Press, 1993), 33.

30. Ibid., 82–83.

31. Glisson, 233.

32. Ransby, 188.

33. Ibid., 176.

34. Glisson, 176.

35. Library of Virginia, "Ella Josephine Baker—African American Trailblazers," March 5, 2009, https://www.youtube.com/watch?v=73Z87y6OgGc, accessed February 18, 2019.

36. Ransby, 22.

37. Ibid., 23.

38. Carey, 27.

39. Judith Weisenfeld, *African American Women and Christian Activism: New York's Black YWCA, 1905–1945* (Cambridge, MA: Harvard University Press, 1997), 37–38.

40. Ibid., 38.

41. Ibid., 10.

42. Dorothy Height, *Open Wide the Freedom Gates: A Memoir* (New York: Public Affairs, 2003), 15.

43. Ibid., 28.

44. Toni C. King and S. Alease Ferguson, eds., *Black Womanist Leadership: Tracing the Motherline* (Albany: State University of New York Press, 2010), 233.

45. Luke 12:48.

CHAPTER 6

Then My Living Will Not Be in Vain

"You intended to harm me, but God intended it for good to accomplish what is now being done, the saving of many lives."[1] Joseph shared these words with his brothers when they feared his retribution for all they had done to him years before. He had suffered greatly, yet Joseph recognized that God had used his hardships to position him to save nations from starvation. In the crucible of his trials, God formed Joseph into a transforming agent for God's purposes.

Consider the progression: Joseph started life as a well-loved, favored son of a family who had sufficient provision for their well-being. But being sold to Midianites, Joseph learned what it meant to live a nomad's life, needing to travel for provision. Later, having been sold into household slavery, Joseph learned what it meant to be a servant whose life was bound to someone else. But through this experience, Joseph learned how to manage a household and its staff, leveraging those lessons to help Potiphar to flourish. His encounter with Potiphar's wife exposed him to the pain of false accusations which led to imprisonment for attempted rape. However, his imprisonment enabled him to relate to those who were imprisoned and the unique conditions of their plight. Additionally, his experiences allowed him to learn how to care for and lead prisoners because the chief jailer entrusted people to Joseph's supervision. This leadership position provided the opportunity for Joseph to meet the king's imprisoned cup bearer and baker to interpret their dreams. In time, the cup bearer remembered Joseph and his giftedness when Pharaoh experienced dreams that he did not understand. By interpreting Pharaoh's dreams, Joseph found favor with Pharaoh and was given authority over all of Egypt.

So, we see the example of hardship being turned into lessons for learning. However, God's grace is the underlying theme of this story. By God's grace, Joseph's brothers did not kill him as was initially suggested even though they were jealous of him. God's grace was with Joseph when he managed Potiphar's household and when he served the chief jailer, as evidenced by the prosperity of both men, who benefited from Joseph's leadership. God's grace was with Joseph when he met with Pharaoh and interpreted his dreams. And God's grace was with Joseph as God prospered Joseph's plan to store surplus grain during the seven years of plentiful harvests. Joseph's plan saved Egypt and the bordering countries during the seven years of famine that struck the land. God's grace restored Joseph and allowed him to forgive, which was seen through the naming of his children. "Joseph named the firstborn Manasseh, 'For,' he said, 'God has made me forget all my hardship and all my father's house.' The second he named Ephraim, 'For God has made me fruitful in the land of my misfortunes.'"[2] Joseph's restoration was the result of grace, but there was much more to it than that. All of Joseph's experiences, both positive and negative, were combined and leveraged so that, through God, Joseph knew how to lead effectively. With a full heart and the benefit of reflection, Joseph recognized that all he had been through was meant for good.

I believe the experiences of African American women parallel those of Joseph, and believing in that parallel relationship, I also believe God has meant these experiences for good, to save numerous peoples. People of African descent were stolen from their homeland and enslaved for the benefit of others. African Americans in general, and women more specifically, suffered through enslavement, exploitation, and disenfranchisement for hundreds of years in this country. In the present day, African American women continue to suffer from discriminatory practices that relegate them to the lowest wages and to restrictive opportunities, even though they have distinguished themselves as some of the most educationally qualified candidates in the labor market. By holding on to faith as a core practice, African

American women have recognized the restorative power of grace and have used that power to learn from their experiences. The lessons learned allowed African American women to survive and thrive in all environments. However, as these lessons are channeled toward our communities, I believe these experiences have the capacity to save because the leadership required for flourishing is communicable. Moreover, as these lessons are employed, they have the capacity to transform our communities for the good. All that is necessary is to glean from the narratives and take the reflective time to understand the lessons of leadership embedded in the African American woman's story. These are stories of effectiveness in leadership, demonstrating how African American women subverted oppression to realize a model from which others can learn. In this chapter, I want to make those lessons plain so all might benefit from them.

For me, it starts with leadership and how to realize effectiveness. In *Spiritual Practices for Effective Leadership: 7 Rs of Sanctuary for Pastors*, I defined leadership as the task of inspiring and mobilizing others to engage actively in the learning required to address competently the challenges that an organization faces.[3] The crux of leadership in this definition is the ability to mobilize others to actively engage them, which is the challenge of efficacy. People typically feel self-efficacious, which is that capacity to be self-governing and exhibit confidence in one's ability to get a job done. But it is more challenging to encourage and inspire efficacy in others. However, as my research demonstrated, if leaders can create a holding environment in which productive pressure and energy are generated for team engagement and interaction, then effectiveness is realized. It is in that holding environment where the work gets done.

An effective leader knows how to modulate the temperature in that environment, creating enough urgency to foster collaborative working conditions. Leaders do this by using emotional intelligence, the strategies that generate positive or negative resonating responses, to motivate learning and innovation. I remember utilizing both tactics with engineering teams. At times, I would employ positive incentives, supportive accolades, and friendly competitions to boost performance. Other times, my actions were punitive, such as when I told my team no one was going home until a system on which we were working was operational. Effective leaders know which strategies to use, but they must learn how to deploy these strategies while maintaining a self-differentiated, non-anxious presence. Such a strategy helps the leader hold the space for team functioning without getting caught up in the generated anxiety. Realizing effectiveness in leadership through these strategies is challenging because it is predicated on one's ability to inspire efficacy in others. As a result, reflective practice is the primary recommendation for leaders because it enables leaders to become self-differentiated and non-anxious, which in turn helps them to create effectively and to modulate the team's holding environment for productive results.

Although the goal of the 7 Rs is leadership effectiveness, the process is primarily focused on equipping the leader. Through reflective practice, leaders are equipped because they learn how to become self-differentiated. They also learn now to create the holding environment that enables the active and collective engagement of teams. But reflective practice also provides opportunity for introspection for the leader. As we reflect, we can see who we are, who God wants us to be, and how to become our best selves. This was my experience. What I learned most notably as I reflected was that my ways of leading as a black woman did not exactly align with what noted leadership strategies or theorists suggested. And from this experience, I concluded that my ways of leading were not in the book.

I had my own methods of creating a holding environment and developing high-performing teams. These methods were born of my experiences as an African American woman working in overwhelmingly male-dominated environments. Initially, I did not think them unique, trivializing them instead as tactics that I had to employ as an African American woman. However, in community with other women who acknowledged employing similar methods, I came to appreciate my faith-based, culturally curated, community-advocating ways of leading. They did not fit the norms, but they worked for me. The same was true for many of the woman with whom I spoke. They expressed the challenges of rising above restrictive systems that did not seem to value their knowledge or expertise. Yet, through their efforts, they were finding ways to thrive and succeed as leaders. By reflecting on the narratives of African American women, what emerged for me was a model of womanist leadership that more accurately spoke to how African American women have lived, led, and survived. Like Joseph, the lessons from experiences were hard-wrought. But they are for good because the experiences yield a way of effective leading. The Model of Womanist Leadership (see figure 1) results from the lessons of African American women, given their lived experiences. It is anchored by faith, expanded by intersectional perspectives, and girded by counterhegemonic strategies, which cooperate to overcome oppressions. Moreover, the focus of this model is community as the chief benefactor, which is transformative.

Figure 1: Model of Womanist Leadership

A Foundation of Faith

At the foundation of this model of womanist leadership is faith. African American women are the most religiously adherent people in the United States, and from that fact, we recognize faith in God plays a key role for African American women as a core belief. Furthermore, faith takes on many dimensions in its practice. As noted in chapter 3, African American women express faith in a God who is on their side. They also express faith in Jesus as a Messiah who personally identifies with them as most marginalized. So, God is seen as one who intercedes for African American women, extending grace and favor, which guards and sustains them through any situation. With belief in such an interceding God, African American women exercise faith in their ability to discern God's leading in various circumstances. Reflection, for example, opens us to the power of discernment, where we can sense how God is moving and faithfully progress with the guidance of God's Spirit. Through prayer and meditation, people of faith speak of discerning God's Spirit, sensing excitement or trepidation as they consider God's leading. But the focus is not necessarily on making the "right" choice. The experience of African American women confirms faith in a God who will never leave or forsake. As the psalmist said in Psalm 139:8, whether I ascend to heaven or make my bed in Sheol, God is there. The same God who African American women trust to be on their side is the one who will guide them through whatever path they follow.

Yet the foundation of faith extends beyond faith in a higher power. African American women have been built up with a faith in self. Growing up as a minority in the United States challenges one's self-esteem because it is difficult to find affirmation in difference. As a teenager growing up in a predominantly white community in the Midwest, I did not understand why boys were interested in my friends but not me. I naïvely believed that being slightly chubby was the cause. Even when a new African American boy moved to the school and all my friends conspired to match the two of us, it did not occur to me that race was an issue. But it was. At times it was as subtle as not having a partner at a school dance. At other times, my difference was made blatantly obvious by those who would refer to me as the N-word, demonstrating that they wanted nothing to do with me. Add to these examples the fact that African American women did not see affirming examples of themselves in print, movies, or television. Few advertisements or mass-media articles promoted African American beauty or esteemed African American norms as positive.

Therefore, family and community serve as the course correctors for African American children. Parents and extended families pour into children letting them know they are valued, special, and esteemed. I recently preached a sermon to a black church congregation, sharing with them that as children of God they are a chosen and royal priesthood. It might seem trivial, but people need to hear that they have value and importance. As those messages are reinforced, people begin to realize faith in themselves. My parents instilled in me that I could do anything I set my mind to doing. My grandparents affirmed I was gifted. Aunts and uncles told me I was attractive. Neighbors said they were proud of me, but so too did strangers. When I graduated with my engineering degree, a black woman ran to me saying, "I know you don't know me, but you're the only person on that stage who looked like me, so I wanted to congratulate you." This is what African American families and communities did and continue to do for their people. By building them up, people are affirmed in their faith and in themselves.

With that affirmation I can embrace a faith in self. Women commonly suffer from imposter syndrome. It is a fear, often unfounded, where women believe themselves to be less capable than others. In that space of self-doubt, women fear others will discover they are not as smart. It is a paralyzing condition that creates reticence and is observed in the job market. For example, a statistic suggests that men apply for a job when they meet 60 percent of qualifications, while women only apply when they meet them 100 percent.[4] Women tend to doubt what they know because they lack confidence in their abilities, which creates uncertainty. I remember being invited to serve on the board of directors of a nonprofit organization. Having a lofty perception of what board leadership meant, I was nervous. Why did they pick me? What could I possibly contribute? Surely someone had made a mistake. Not only was I fearful of being discovered as an imposter, but also I was suffering from an overactive sense of inadequacy. These fears nearly caused me to decline the invitation.

Nevertheless, I attended my first board meeting, and it was a startling event. What I learned in that meeting was that my peer board member colleagues were no smarter than I. In fact, I quickly realized some were not as smart. I had been convinced I did not belong and was disavowed of that opinion only by having experienced the meeting. Socialization and opportunity were the differentiators. My colleagues, particularly those who were white men, had been socialized to believe they deserved a place at the table and given the chance to capitalize on the opportunity. I did not have that same socialization or opportunity, and that lack created in me anxiety that I did not belong. But through the faith instilled by family, community, and church, I was able to draw upon all that was poured into me, coupling those affirmations with individual experiences, both positive and negative, to overcome my fears and exercise faith in my abilities.

My sense of self-efficacy has only grown with increasing faith in my abilities. Far from conceit, my confidence is rooted in faith, for I believe I can do all things through Christ who strengthens me. It is an amazing sense of knowing and feeling exonerated in that knowledge. Such self-confidence has ties to feminist standpoint theory while also linking to my family history. Feminist standpoint theory affirms that my knowledge has value, and it does not matter that the value may be derived from a culturally specific viewpoint. That knowledge is of value notwithstanding.

To illustrate, there is a recipe for caramel cake frosting has been passed down in my family for generations. This seemingly simple recipe calls for butter, sugar, and evaporated milk to be simmered over low heat to reach a required temperature and consistency. Properly prepared, the recipe makes a delicious caramelized frosting that is sumptuous over cake. Improperly prepared, the recipe yields a sticky, useless mess. The women of my family who made this recipe knew without measuring what was required. They knew the right amounts of ingredients, and they knew from observing the mixture boiling when the correct temperature had been reached. They simply knew. They had no measuring utensils or thermometers, but they were confident in their knowledge. In their context, their knowledge had value. They may not have known great mysteries of the world. They may not have had educational opportunities that I was privileged to receive. However, my knowledge made them no less confident in their knowledge. Those family members who came before me were rooted in the knowledge they gained through experience, and that kind of confidence instills faith.

And the same is true for African American women, which is why the model of womanist leadership begins with faith at its foundation. For African American Christian women, it is faith in God through Jesus Christ. But it is a faith that is extended to self because of the nurture of family and community. Because African American families and communities have cooperated to build up their children, children grow to realize faith in others and in themselves. Moreover, African American women have leveraged that faith to exhibit confidence in what they know. Such faith has served to undergird African American women because faith builds the individual to overcome societies and socializations that destroy and undermine confidence. As women have operated in that foundation of faith, they are able to extend the same sense of faith and confidence in others. I am most cognizant of this when I engage young girls in church. When I meet a young girl, I intentionally speak to her, dropping to a knee if necessary and making eye contact, which is affirming. I want her to know how special she is. I want her to see herself in me and draw strength that increases her faith in self. It is a lesson that womanist leaders can easily exercise if we first have that sense of confident faith in ourselves.

Years ago, I had a manager say to me, "A-players attract A-players; B-players attract C-players." He was saying that when you are confident in who you are, you are not intimidated by others who are equally confident, and you will welcome them on your team. However, if you are lacking in self-confidence, you will attract those you deem less capable so they are not a threat. But such a practice creates suboptimal teams that cannot perform at exceptional levels of proficiency and productivity. Through a foundation of faith, leaders can help to stave off such performance limitations. It is a westernized leadership model that wants to elevate the leader as the smartest or most-competent member of the team. But a womanist leadership model draws confidence from knowledge in self that is rooted in faith. Just as the apostle Paul noted the diversity of gifts given by God through the Holy Spirit, so leaders need to recognize that a diversity of gifts exists in the team. A more-esteemed gift does not make it greater. I do not have to be the smartest person on the team. I have faith and confidence in what I know and can contribute. Thus, freed from the angst of having to be the smartest, I can focus my efforts on assembling the smartest and most-capable people into a collaborative and high-performing unit. Then I am adding value and living into my role as a leader. Specifically, I use my abilities to inspire and mobilize others to engage actively in the learning required to address competently the challenges that an organization faces, which is my definition of leadership. It begins with a foundation of faith in God, self, and others.

Expanded Focus through an Intersectional Standpoint

A womanist leadership model features an intersectional standpoint, which includes the recognition of multiple oppressions, increased awareness, and an expanded dialectical perspective that helps African American women navigate their environments. The impact of interrelated systems of oppression is multilayered and impossible to confront in isolation. Nevertheless, oppressions can have a natural order that uniquely affects women of color, who will first be prejudged by the basis of their skin. In a color-conscious society, race is immediately recognized as a discriminator, not to differentiate between, but rather as a tool of subordination. Since the first European explorers came to Africa, color has been used to elevate those who were regarded as white over those who were not. Those who were deemed closest to the white standard were esteemed higher than those who were not. Thus, to be black, which was the antithesis of whiteness, was an oppressive stigma. It was a glaringly obvious stigma, but not the only one.

The female gender, which is often second in its ordering, was also detrimental. If we attempt to view the challenge of gender in isolation, we readily recognize oppression. Consider, for example, the view of the conservative church that believes in the biblical mandate to subordinate women because of the fall of humanity. Such justification continues to motivate the prohibition of women's leadership in the church. Drawing upon a hodgepodge of selective biblical texts that suggest subordination and silence, woman's voices and leadership are justifiably marginalized. But the church is only a microcosm of a broader society that also marginalizes women by confining them to relegated and subordinated roles. Such practices explain why so many of our churches and organizations which have been made productive by women are led by men. The efforts of women are needed, but they are discouraged from leading. It is said that if it were not for the women, we would not have the church. This truism can be said in a variety of contexts, and still women continue to be subordinated.

Yet African American women suffer gender-based discrimination differently than white women. Sojourner Truth spoke of a distinguishing difference in her remarks from the 1851 Women's Rights Convention in Akron, Ohio, now famously captured in "Ain't I a Woman?" She acknowledged a man who suggested that women needed to be helped into carriages, lifted over ditches, and enjoy the best places. A sexist construct concluded that women, in their frailty, needed the assistance of a man. However, as a woman, Sojourner noted that no such courtesies had been extended to her. Instead, her status as a black woman condemned her to hardship—watching her children sold into slavery, laboring at the same level of productivity as a man and suffering the abuse. She was not esteemed for her gender but rather subjected to a harsher double indictment as black and as a black woman.

The impact of race and gender is further complicated by the oppressions related to class, which is why some authors speak of the triple jeopardy of being an African American woman. Being an African American woman has a direct effect on one's socioeconomic outcome, because race and gender conspire to limit socioeconomic mobility. African American women make less money than white men, women, and African American men. They are afforded fewer opportunities for advancement. But regardless of education or experience, often they had to accept what was offered for lack of alternative options. Particularly in times of economic downturn, African American women have been exploited for their labor, in some instances accepting only pennies per day because they had families to feed and bills that were due. African American women were also exploited for their ignorance, which similarly conspired to limit economic potential and mobility. It was the reality of the concrete ceiling that the blocked knowledge of expanded possibilities, leaving African American women at a distinct disadvantage because they were simply unaware.

The knowledge of these interlocking oppressive systems provides African American women with the widest possible view of one's context, rather than a narrowed and privileged perspective. As a left-handed individual, I readily recognize the number of appliances that are made for right-handed people. For example, most microwaves assume that users will open the door of the oven with their left hand and operate controls with their right. But this is true of several daily-use items that are so oriented. Even something as simple as an ink pen assumes right-handedness because the labeling on the pen is positioned to be read properly when holding the pen with one's right hand.

As an African American woman, I recognize the same biases in leadership. As an engineering leader, I was esteemed more when I functioned utilizing traditionally male leadership characteristics. This preference for male leadership is particularly true in faith communities. Female colleagues who are co-rabbis shared that when they solicited input from their congregation for a new cantor, feedback included comments saying the cantor needed to have a tenor voice. It was an obvious expression of preference. Even something as innocuous as finding clergy garb is difficult because a male clerical norm means that robes are too large and stoles are too long. So, my perspective is not narrow when I confront social systems. I can recognize the system as it operates and as it oppresses. This means that women, for example, understand how men operate in a male-dominated system. Knowing that they cannot function as men, they learn alternative ways. That is what an intersectional standpoint provides: an expanded awareness of others' viewpoints while providing a self-awareness of one's own viewpoint and perspective.

This expanded perspective enables African American women to have greater awareness and empathy for other standpoints. Knowing the impact, African American women recognize these challenges for others who are also oppressed. Solidarity is realized in shared rather than identical experience of oppression, engendering a compassionate receptivity to and advocacy for those who are also oppressed. That sense of solidarity explains why African American women have often felt compelled to speak out for others even when the plight is not personally shared. This is how an intersectional standpoint paves the way for an expanded dialectical perspective. Because African American women are subjected to intersecting oppressions and have been the victims of prejudicial attitudes and actions, they are often best positioned to challenge preconceived notions in the dominant culture.

For example, a society might blame minorities for the depressed conditions of their community, associating ethnicity with poverty. However, utilizing a dialectical method, one might conversely argue there are fewer job opportunities, a lack of quality schools, and limited new development efforts in minority neighborhoods, which conspire to decrease opportunities and depress conditions. People who have been oppressed can offer such arguments because they understand oppression, and they understand the unjust conclusions that are developed as a result. Therefore, by leveraging that intersectional standpoint and engaging in an expanded dialectical perspective, African American women are uniquely positioned to challenge held beliefs and help others realize a more expansive, inclusive viewpoint.

Girding Strategies

African American women also recognize from their experiences that oppressive systems are dehumanizing. Discriminatory and oppressive tactics strip away human dignity as they promote some at the expense of others. A dichotomy is created that deems one as good and another as bad. If, for example, straight hair, light complexion, blue eyes, and a European body type are beautiful, then coarse hair, dark complexion, brown eyes, and African body type must be ugly. These are the messages that have been overtly and covertly delivered, and unfortunately, many African American women and girls have been hurt by them. Thus, in addition to challenging negative stereotypes through dialectical methods, African American women have had to adopt strategies for self-preservation. Such girding strategies represent counterhegemonic movements. Hegemony speaks to a dominant way of viewing or doing things. So, when the dominant culture defined black as bad, to be black was offensive. At least this was the view for African Americans who were Negros in the mid twentieth century. For my grandmother's generation, given the cultural climate and indoctrination, to be called black was the highest insult possible. For me, to be called black is not offensive, but it does point out otherness, which, especially during my formative years, was problematic. I remember when my fifth-grade math teacher once pulled me aside and said, "Black is beautiful, and you are beautiful." I now understand he wanted to affirm me, but at the time, I was mortified. How could he make such a public example of me in front of my classmates? I was embarrassed then, but I came to appreciate that he was attempting to gird me with affirmations to challenge a negative narrative.

Specifically, if black was synonymous with bad and deemed ugly, then to declare "black is beautiful" was counterhegemonic. The labeling that was given to oppress and marginalize could be subverted and converted to an affirmation that would empower. African American people learned to do this for themselves on numerous levels. As chapter 4 noted, Africans were disparaged for their shiny, greasy appearance, and African American men and boys were mocked and called "shines." To exploit and make fun of difference is a hegemonic move, but African American college students subverted the meaning, declaring "shine" as a reference to their brilliance. To say "pardon my blackness, I didn't mean to shine" was counterhegemonic. Not only does it declare an inherent value in being black, but also it recognizes that to shine is to allow your talents to show forth. The fashion industry often identifies African American bodies as nonconforming with the differences deemed as less than the ideal norm. But African Americans have subverted these ideas of fashion inferiority. African American women have learned to recognize and celebrate their bodies, and through a self-aware love, appreciate their beauty. Additionally, they have learned to use what their mommas gave them to claim boldly and live into their identities. One of the most iconic African American clothing lines, FUBU, celebrates clothing that is "For Us By Us."

African American women also have taken advantage of the fact that they will be undervalued or relegated to invisibility in social situations. Again, this is a countercultural response that results from multiple oppressions. Both African Americans and women are undervalued in this culture, and the combination renders African American women as indistinguishable from others. But I am amazed by the number of women in leadership situations who have parlayed invisibility into a strength. I facilitated a panel discussion of African American women leaders who included a senior vice president of a Fortune 100 company, a regional banker who managed more than $500 million in assets, a neuroscientist and university dean, and a university chief diversity officer. Each woman spoke of occasions where she was underestimated and disregarded in group settings. Yet they all used the misjudgment to observe quietly, assessing the situation, sizing up the participants, and discerning choices. In each case, people seemed shocked by their brilliance. No one expected these women to have anything of value to say. Theirs was a counterhegemonic strategy: leverage the underestimation and ultimately dictate the direction of the discussion. There was pride in the retelling of these stories, but the women were not operating with the intent of gaining superiority or attempting to make those who had undervalued them look badly. Rather they were asserting and preserving their personal self-worth. They were effectively saying, "I have something to contribute." Grounded by faith, expanded by intersectional standpoint, and emboldened by girding strategies that subvert the hegemonic movements, African American women have learned to function with power and conviction. These practices are indicative of a womanist leadership model.

Focus on Community

These practices must have an end to which their energies are directed. For African American women, the trajectory points to community, which is the key culminating point because community holds great affinity. The loyalty to community stems from African culture, which reinforced the power and strength of community. This cultural imprint remained with people of the African diaspora and is evident through the lives of African American women. Learning and nurturing happened in community. People learned to relate and find purpose in community. And given the challenges weathered by African Americans through their four-hundred-year history in the United States, community served as an anchor, and the definition was expanded to be inclusive of a variety of communal spaces: home, extended family, the church, or geographic area. Communal connections were a part of life, and women leveraged those connections significantly. As noted in the preceding chapters, women formed communities to raise funds, educate, serve, advocate, and make connections. It was a dynamic formation and widely inclusive. Club women saw themselves as community, as did church women. But African American women also made themselves part of communities where they lived or worked, which explains why some women who served as domestics during the mid twentieth century were regarded as part of the family. And being a part of the community in which they functioned, they gave back to that community. An ethic of service characterized communal responsibility and was imparted to African American women. Not only did they learn to serve the community, but also they taught their children, providing a framework that encouraged and perpetuated communal involvement.

Furthermore, recognizing the collective power of communal involvement and service, I contend that African American women are less likely to aspire to individual recognition. It is more important to be a contributing, productive member of the community. The women I profiled, from Mary Church Terrell and Nannie Helen Burroughs, to Ella Baker and Dorothy Height, each demonstrated this. They recognized a responsibility to give back and extended themselves in ways that were not self-serving. In fact, their names are largely unknown in the broader society because of their unsung background efforts, a stunning reality given the tremendous impact of their work. How else do we describe someone like Ella Baker, who is arguably the greatest civil rights champion of whom too few have heard? In an age that promotes self-aggrandizement, her actions epitomize a countercultural response because she sought no credit. She eschewed the spotlight. But her actions embody what it means to be a womanist leader.

Service to community is important, and esteeming others through efforts that lift all is more important than self. Such selfless service is transformational. African American women, being raised and nurtured in community, recognize benefit from the community. They in turn serve their communities and encourage others under their leadership to serve similarly. The expanded view of community makes this possible. Having been raised and nurtured in the church, I now seek to raise and nurture others in the church. As a woman in ministry, having been helped by a community of women in ministry, I now mentor other women in ministry, who likewise have become mentors. That is the hope of transformation: those who have been transformed will then work to transform others. Thus, this model promotes transformational communal impact.

However, the model is operational as well. Womanism constitutes a way of being in the world, and leadership serves as the practical application of our being. Therefore, womanist leadership is a way of leveraging womanist traits such as a foundation of faith, inclusivity, and a culture of care in ways that foster communal transformation. According to Alice Walker in *In Search of Our Mother's Gardens*, a womanist is committed to the survival and wholeness of an entire people. A womanist is not interested in separatism, and advocates instead for a universality that is inclusive of everyone. Moreover, a womanist is oriented toward caring for others, doing all that can be done to make a difference. By assuming the mantle of leadership, African American women actualize these characteristics and bring them to bear in community.

It is important to note, however, that African American women do not necessarily recognize or esteem that exercise of leadership in traditional ways. As was taught by the women who came before them, they often exercise leadership in quiet, background ways. This is a unique aspect of womanist leadership. Society reinforces that the one out front and in control is to be recognized and esteemed as the leader. But this is not the model of leadership so many African American women have assumed. Of course, there are those who have been out front, and their names are known. Yet countless others are unknown. These were the women who banded together to fund a church mission, positively engage children after school, or sit in the galleries of public hearings to demand services. Their model of leadership sought strategies to advocate for all. Moreover, their exercise of leadership evolved and adapted as was needed for a situation. An expanded intersectional standpoint enables such adaptability. We might understand and define these styles as masculine or feminine leadership, servant leadership, or community-centered leadership, but the labeling never mattered to African American women. Grounded, girded, and aware of their environment, African American women have employed the tools that were most effective for the benefit of those in their community.

The Transformational Power of Womanist Leadership

What would our organizations look like if more leaders operated in such selfless ways? What if we as leaders, being rooted and grounded in our faith and values, sought to include others in our decision making, drawing in diverse opinions? What if we tried to be as expansive and inclusive as possible in developing the strategies that maximized flourishing for all? What if we employed tactics that would invert operational structures and restore human dignity rather than exploit? What if our efforts as leaders were truly about changing and positively affecting our communities? Would it not be of value to harness such a leadership style?

I am convinced that leading from this womanist framework has the power to change our communities for the good because there is much to commend. A model that has faith at its foundation builds resiliency. For me, it is a faith in God through Jesus Christ, but a universal definition of faith is not required. The act of believing creates capacity for hope. It allows us to endure confidently. And with that capacity, we can weather the challenges and difficulties in our lives. The four-hundred-year history of African American women in this country stands in testament. Because of their faith, African American women survived. In fact, we have been able to persevere regardless of the circumstance. And as leaders, we need to be rooted and anchored in a faith that enables us to be similarly resilient.

An intersectional standpoint increases one's perspective. I once heard a business school professor declare that fish do not know they are swimming in water; it is just part of the environment. Privilege similarly blunts our sensitivities. It is so easy to take for granted the things we have that we hardly stop to consider the perspective of others. But when you are confronted with bias and prejudice just because of who you are, what you believe, or who you love, it heightens sensitivity and increases awareness. We all need these skills in this age. We need to be able to engage people where they are so we can serve with and make a difference together. An intersectional standpoint achieves this because it helps us to be more expansive and inclusive. It helps us to value people, not in their otherness, but in their humanity.

Girding strategies subvert the status quo. I met a leader who shared the story of saving his failing family business. The story in its introduction had all the markings of the great man narrative: the conquering hero who would come to save the day, righting the wrongs of previous leaders. But that was not how the story went. Recognizing an inability to admit wrongdoing as a core failure of the company, he set out to help people embrace transparency and modeled a willingness to admit when he messed up. He worked with his leaders to recast a vision for the organization that would deal truthfully and respectfully with one another as employees and with the franchisees, partners, and customers who were impacted by the business. Human dignity became the motivating value over profits or competitive advantage. The practices he encouraged were countercultural to the operating norms of the industry, and yet they took root. Moreover, these changes restored confidence in the company. When this leader admitted the many corporate misdeeds and examples of maleficence, the franchisees agreed to negotiate a settlement rather than sue. Who would imagine that doing the right thing and valuing human dignity was a subversive strategy? But through subversion, this company became stronger and more successful than it had ever been.

Most importantly, the community benefits when this model is engaged. Jesus told his disciples that he came to serve, not to be served. I believe this should be our mantra as leaders as well. Leadership is about making a positive difference, and our gifting as leaders helps us to do that. I used to tell my teams that leadership was like a kit bag filled with tools. My job was to solicit inputs, assess situations, and then determine what tool was most applicable for the task at hand. Additionally, my job was to clear obstacles so others could excel. Ultimately, if the team succeeded, then I heralded them as the champions, but if the team failed, I took the blame because I was the leader.

The model of womanist leadership encapsulates how I have led. My experiences, perspectives, and girding have come together in ways that allowed me to draw from my resources for the benefit of the community. But it also exhibits what I pray is a way of being and leading that is oriented toward others and not self. Girded and affirmed, it is a way of leading that does not mind being provocative for the cause of others. Expansively inclusive, it is a way of leading that builds up and does not tear down. Rooted in faith, it is a way of leading that persists. Robert Greenleaf said the result of servant leadership is that those being served become healthier, wiser, freer, more autonomous, and more likely to become servants. I do not know whether womanist leadership would make such a claim. However, in the words of an old hymn of the black church, a womanist leader would simply assert, "If I can help somebody as I pass along, then my living will not be in vain."

I was captured and motivated by the quote of researchers Darlene Clark Hine and Kathleen Thompson who said, "The values that have helped Black women survive are entirely communicable. And at a time when the problems of our society seem insoluble and the obstacles to peace and freedom insurmountable, all Americans have a great deal to learn from the history of black women in America."[5] But I am also struck by the way of learning, which is not a step-by-step methodology. The lessons in leadership are learned from the matrilineal narratives. This is not to say that men do not have contributions or that their stories are unimportant. But we always hear his-story. It is time to hear her-story. Besides, as has been demonstrated, the ways that African American women have led were not recognized as leadership. Therefore, if we would listen to their stories with an expanded perspective, we can glean for ourselves unique ways of leadership, possibly countercultural or subversive but always directed at making a difference in our communities, which is transforming because it fosters continuing service. It is womanist leadership that gleans stories to bolster faith, expand standpoints, and strengthen itself with girding strategies, promoting communal engagement for the benefit of all. And God meant it for good.

Notes
1. Genesis 50:20, NIV.
2. Genesis 41:51-52.
3. Debora Jackson, *Spiritual Practices for Effective Leadership: 7 Rs of Sanctuary for Pastors* (Valley Forge, PA: Judson Press, 2015), 7.
4. Tara Sophia Mohr, "Why Women Don't Apply for Jobs Unless They Are 100% Qualified," *Harvard Business Review*, August 25, 2014, https://hbr.org/2014/08/why-women-dont-apply-for-jobs-unless-theyre-100-qualified, accessed February 25, 2019.
5. Darlene Clark Hine and Kathleen Thompson, *A Shining Thread of Hope: The History of Black Women in America* (New York: Broadway Books, 1998), 308.

Index

A

Abram, 56

"acting white," 97

Acts 2:44-45, 105

advocacy/advocating, 120, 126
  African American men and, 109
  community, 132
  for oneself, 15, 22, 47
  home training and, 93
  inspiring, 119–122
  justice, 23, 64
  promoting, 111
  promoting equity through, 105–106
  for inclusion, 146
  unmasking systems of injustice, 119
  vocal, 94

affirmation
  "black is beautiful," 142–143
  creating a culture that encourages, 47–48
  empowering, 143

African(s),
  abuse of, 30
  advocacy efforts, 109
  beauty, 27–29, 135, 142–143
  cultural awareness, 26
  culture, pride in, 40
  diaspora, 26, 40, 56
  European's negative perception of, 27–28
  "Hottentots," 28
  Joseph and the Pharaoh story in relation to, 130–131
  justifiable discrimination, 29–30, 84
  Khoisan women, 28–29
  public displays of punishment, 109
  religion/belief systems, 105

stereotypes regarding, 28, 30–33
support systems, 43, 81
survival tactics, 106
violence against, 108–109

African American women
  advocating for oneself, 15
  assertiveness in, 11
  Biblical narrative and, 55–59
  body image, 27–29, 31, 33–34, 36–39, 41–42, 45–48
  church attendance, 61, 66–68, 72
  civil rights movement and, 110–122, 145
  communal practices, 106, 145
  cultural awareness, 26
  cultural experiences of, 15, 16
  defense mechanisms, 99–100
  discrimination against, 34–37, 63, 84, 130
  dualities, 15
  education, 63, 73–74, 84–87, 90–91, 95–102, 130, 140
  employment, 44, 63, 75, 90, 114, 130
  expectations of, 86–87, 90, 143–144
  faith/religious affiliation, 51–77, 130, 134–138
  "fallen womanhood," 30–31
  fashion industry and, 34, 41–42
  feminist standpoint theory and, 13
  girding strategies, 142–144, 146, 148
  hair, 37, 43
  Jesus, relationship to, 57–58, 134, 137
  leadership, 11, 12, 16, 20, 32–33, 38, 42–50, 75, 91, 94–101, 109, 112, 115, 132
  leadership, theory of, 12–16

Index

shoes
  slaves', 104
  status of having, 104
  symbolism of, 125–126
Shulamite woman, 39 53
skin bleaching, 37
skin color, 37–39, 96
slavery, 30, 56–57, 87, 130
  children born into, 57, 139
  Christianity and, 52–53, 104–105
  distortion of the Bible during, 53
  education and, 93
  faith/religious affiliation and, 51–52
  justification for, 84–85
  legacy of, 9
  masters, 105
  mixed-race children as a result
    of rape, 32, 57
  religious practices of new slaves, 105
  shoes and clothes for slaves, 104
  women and, 30–32, 139–140
Smith, Christine, 67
Social independence, 124
Social justice consciousness, 124–126
societal preferences, 39
  Shulamite woman, 39, 53
Southern Christian Leadership Confer
  ence (SCLC), 111–113, 117–118
    guiding principles, 113–122
    leaders, 118
Southern folk culture, 113
Spiritual Practices for Effective
  Leadership: 7Rs of Sanctuary for
  Pastors (Jackson), 131
Sports Illustrated, 41
standpoint
  African American women, 14, 19
  expanding, 126
  feminist, 12–14
  intersectional, 138–142, 147
  multiple, 20
narrative, claiming, 22
  theory, 12–14, 115
  understanding, 19
  womanist, 17

"Steal Away to Jesus," 55
Stereotypes
  Africans, 28, 30–33
  African Americans and education, 89
  African American women, 30–37,
    40–41, 44, 48, 84, 89, 94
  "angry black woman," 4, 33, 36
  body image, 40
  conforming, 44
  contributing to marginalization,
    44, 48
  embracing, 14
  inverting, 40
  limiting, 14
  overcoming/subverting, 14, 48, 91
  reinforcing, 35–36, 44
street evangelism, 75
student activism, 113
Student Nonviolent Coordinating
  Council, 64, 113
Supreme Court, 11
Systema naturae (Linnaeus), 81

T

tent meetings, 75
Terrell, Robert, 88
"That's Why They Call Me Shine"
  (Dabney and Mack), 82
theory of dissemblance, 99–100
Thomas, Clarence, 11
Thompson, Kathleen, 149
Thurman, Howard, 52–53, 58
Time for Honor: A Portrait of African
  American Clergywomen
  (Carpenter), 71
Truth, Sojourner, 139–140
Turner, Ike, 44
Turner, Tina, 44

U

Unitarian Universalists, 72–73
United Church of Christ, 72–73
United Church of Christ Statistical
  Profile, 72–73
United Council of Negro Women, 89

Index